KANZASHI IN BLOOM

20 Simple
Fold-and-Sew
Projects to
Wear and Give

DIANE
GILLELAND

WATSON-GUPTILL PUBLICATIONS/NEW YORK

KANZASHI
IN BLOOM

For Mom

Text copyright © 2009 by Diane Gilleland
Style photographs copyright © 2009 by Simon Lee
Process photographs copyright © 2009 by Pam Harris

First published in 2009 by Watson-Guptill Publications,
Crown Publishing Group, a division of Random House Inc., New York
www.crownpublishing.com
www.watsonguptill.com

Library of Congress Cataloging-in-Publication Data

Gilleland, Diane.
  Kanzashi in bloom : 20 simple fold-and-sew projects to wear and give / by Diane Gilleland.
     p. cm.
  Includes bibliographical references and index.
  ISBN 978-0-8230-8481-4 (pbk. : alk. paper)
 1. Silk flowers. 2. Decorative arts—Japan. I. Title.

 TT890.7.G45 2009
 745.594'3—dc22

                    2009000292

Executive Editor: Joy Aquilino
Development Editor: Amy Vinchesi
Art Director: Jess Morphew
Designer and Photoshoot Art Director (Still Life): Chin-Yee Lai
Production Director: Alyn Evans

Printed in China

First printing, 2009

2 3 4 5 6 7 8 9 / 15 14 13 12 11 10 09

CONTENTS

INTRODUCTION

I always come back to flowers: Any time I'm learning a new craft technique, I try some flower-based design or pattern to practice on. When I design beautiful objects, floral elements always seem to creep in somewhere. So it's no wonder I fell head-over-heels for *Kanzashi*.

Kanzashi are beautiful Japanese flowers created by folding small squares of silk into petals and then gluing them together. You may have seen Kanzashi adorning the elaborate coiffure of a Japanese geisha, because that's their most traditional use. We're not exactly going to be traditional here, but we are going to learn to make Kanzashi. Actually, it's important to note that Kanzashi are more correctly called *Hana Tsumami Kanzashi*. The Japanese word *Kanzashi* refers to the hair ornaments worn by Japanese women, while *Hana* translates as "flower," and *Tsumami* refers to the process of folding the silk squares to make these flowers. However, as the online crafting community has begun to discover and embrace this craft, folded fabric flowers are often casually referred to simply as *Kanzashi*, and that is how I will refer to them in this book.

Speaking of online crafting, that's where I first discovered Kanzashi. One of the many benefits of the Internet is its power to introduce us to creative ideas from all over the world. I should say, though, that my particular method of making

Kanzashi is quite different from the traditional Japanese method, which you can read more about in the first chapter. As much as I love to watch the traditional process in action, I've also found it a bit challenging to learn. The online crafting community, being the inspiring and creative environment that it is, has found some simpler ways to make Kanzashi, and it's from these methods that I evolved the techniques in this book.

I've taught basic Kanzashi classes for a few years now, and it's always fun to see how besotted my students become with this craft. The flowers are so elaborate and so beautiful that once you discover how simple they are to make, well, that becomes all you want to do. Those classes are really the seeds that started this book. In nearly every class I've taught, the question eventually comes up: "What can you do with these flowers?" In my classes, we usually glue pins and magnets to them, but a world of possibility lies beyond that. I've had a wonderful time dreaming up ways to incorporate Kanzashi into jewelry, clothing, bags, home decor, and gifts, to name but a few applications.

I hope you'll enjoy learning to make your own Kanzashi flowers and that you'll want to cover your world with them!

Origins of the Art Form

Kanzashi is both very old and very new. Look into its history and you'll find a tradition of beautiful hair ornaments stretching back thousands of years in Japan. Today a handful of artisans still practice this art using traditional materials and techniques. Alongside these traditional Kanzashi masters you can also find a new generation of enthusiasts. Some are making flowers the traditional way while some are inventing new methods. This new generation of artists is exuberantly sharing its creations online, helping to spread fresh excitement about Kanzashi around the world.

KANZASHI, THEN AND NOW

Image © Kuniko Kanawa, atelierkanawa.com

Let's begin with a little history. Kanzashi first came into widespread use in Japan during the Edo Period, around 1600. Until that time, Japanese women wore their hair long and straight, sometimes reaching all the way to the floor, in a style known as *taregami*. But the Edo Period brought change in the form of elaborate, upswept hairstyles. Women began to curl, sculpt, and adorn their hair, using decorative combs and pins made from metal or lacquered wood: These ornaments were the first Kanzashi.

At the start of the Edo Period, Japan began urbanizing and trading with foreign countries, which gave craftspeople access to new materials and design influences. As a result, Kanzashi-making reached new heights in terms of color and style, and many different types of Kanzashi flourished. *Bira Bira* Kanzashi, for example, were made on a pronged hairpin, with shiny ornaments that dangled and tinkled in the breeze. *Kushi* Kanzashi were formed on large, rounded hair combs, usually made of tortoiseshell or lacquered wood. And *Kogai*, or "sword," Kanzashi were designed using a rod-and-sheath configuration.

Here is a traditional Tsumami Kanzashi in progress, with pre-folded petals lined up in a pool of rice paste.
Image © Kuniko Kanawa, atelierkanawa.com

Floral Kanzashi (which are called *Hana Kanzashi* in Japan) originated around the middle of the Edo Period. The art began with servants in the imperial court, who made silk flowers as a hobby. These flowers soon found their way onto Kanzashi pins and combs, and new artisans emerged to perfect and develop the technique.

Hana Kanzashi are traditionally made using a method called *tsumami*, which involves pinching fabric. A Kanzashi artisan pinches and

Kanzashi are most commonly seen adorning the hair of geisha and their apprentices, who are known as maiko.
Image © iStockphoto.com/mura

trims small squares of silk to create tiny flower petals. Then, using long tweezers, the artisan soaks each petal in a special rice-starch glue and adheres the petals one at a time to a metal or plastic base until a flower takes shape. It's an art that takes a steady hand and a great deal of practice to master. Hana Tsumami Kanzashi come in an incredible array of colors and styles; they mimic just about every flower that grows in Japan and sometimes take on more vibrant, fanciful forms.

In modern Japan, you'll find Kanzashi being worn primarily by geisha and their apprentices, who are known as *maiko*. Traditionally, maiko wear larger and more complex Kanzashi than mature geisha, and an elaborate system exists that dictates what kind of Kanzashi a maiko may wear as she progresses through the stages of her training. Each month of the year is represented by a specific Kanzashi as well: Maiko wear plum-

Kanzashi flowers also make a lovely addition to modern wardrobes.
Image © Meghan Willett, hanatsukuri.etsy.com

blossom Kanzashi in February, for example, and chrysanthemums in October. Public holidays also dictate specific traditional Kanzashi, such as the cherry blossoms that celebrate *Hanami* (cherry blossom viewing) from March to May.

Kanzashi do exist in modern-day Japan outside of geisha culture. Brides bedeck themselves in traditional kimono and obi (a broad sash) for their wedding ceremony and wear beautiful Kanzashi in their hair. Some women who study traditional Japanese culture will wear Kanzashi to perform tea ceremonies or ikebana (the Japanese art of flower-arranging). And occasionally, a Kanzashi brooch will appear as a fashion accent on the lapel of a young woman in modern dress.

Today there are only fifteen acknowledged Tsumami Kanzashi masters around the world.

Above: One of Kuniko Kanawa's traditional Tsumami Kanzashi.
Image © Kuniko Kanawa, atelierkanawa.com

Many of them are growing older and no longer taking apprentices, so sadly, the Kanzashi tradition is beginning to die out. But a handful of younger artisans are stepping in to preserve this art form. Kuniko Kanawa is one such artist. She grew up immersed in westernized Japanese culture, listening to rock and hip-hop music and wearing jeans and T-shirts. But as a young adult, she became fascinated with kimono and the many other traditions surrounding Japanese dress. It was from this passion that Kanawa learned to make Tsumami Kanzashi in order to create affordable hair accessories to match her kimonos. Her excitement about this art form grew. "As I was making more and more Tsumami Kanzashi, I became eager to pursue this traditional art, since it is now a dying art," she says. "I felt a strong mission to pass it to the future generation."

Kanawa's desire to preserve traditions convinced one of Japan's remaining Tsumami Kanzashi masters to accept her as a student. "This art is dying out in Japan because the majority of modern Japanese do not wear kimonos," says Kanawa. "It's a shame that most of us even do not know how to dress ourselves in a kimono. We must revive kimono culture so that Tsumami Kanzashi and other Japanese culture can survive." With her training complete, Kanawa, who now lives in the United States, makes both traditional and modern Tsumami Kanzashi for customers around the world. Much of her business is devoted to outfitting wedding parties with Kanzashi accessories and serving as a consultant for kimono traditions. She also creates Tsumami Kanzashi pieces for Japanese holidays and dance events.

In her mission to preserve traditional Tsumami Kanzashi culture, Kanawa is tapping into the communication resources of the Internet. She not only sells her modern Kanzashi internationally via an online store but has also produced a number of online videos to share Tsumami Kanzashi and kimono traditions with the world. And down the road, she definitely plans to pass along her skills to the next generation of artisans. Refer to the Resources section for more information about Kuniko Kanawa.

A large lotus flower pin by Kuniko Kanawa.
Image © Kuniko Kanawa, atelierkanawa.com

Materials and Core Techniques

Consider this section your Kanzashi toolbox. First we'll look into the best fabrics, glue, and embellishments to use for the projects in this book. Then we'll learn to make three styles of flower petal, which you can mix and match to make literally hundreds of different styles of Kanzashi. And finally, we'll learn to assemble a basic flower. Armed with this information, you'll be prepared to take on any of the projects in this book, or branch out into your own floral creations—which you probably will want to do, as Kanzashi-making is delightfully addictive.

MATERIALS

One nice thing about the simplified Kanzashi techniques in this book is that you can find pretty much everything you need to make them at your local fabric or craft store. Here's a little rundown on the basic supplies you'll want to have on hand. Some of the projects in this book require a few additional materials, but we'll cover those in the project instructions.

FABRICS

Traditional Kanzashi are made from silk, which gives the flowers a lovely, delicate finish. Silk is a little challenging to work with, however, so here are some tips to consider when you choose a fabric for the simplified Kanzashi in this book.

Start with Cotton. Most of the flowers in this book are made with cotton fabrics. They're easy to fold, hold their shape well, and come in a toe-tingling array of colors and prints. Some specialty fabric lines even have glossy or glittery finishes. I turn to cottons again and again when I make Kanzashi. Cotton fabrics also come in a wide array of weights, so select your fabric wisely: If you're making large flowers (three inches in diameter or larger), then try some heavier quilting cottons. They help larger flowers hold their shapes very well. If you're making small flowers (less than two inches in diameter), then it's better to use the lightest-weight cotton you can find, such as a batik or a

batiste. Thinner cottons like these can take lots of folding without making the finished flowers too bulky. If you're making flowers in the 2 to 3" range, then you can use cotton of just about any weight.

One other nice thing about cotton is that, thanks to the quilting community, many fabric stores are now stocked with "fat quarters," which are generous $1/4$-yard pieces of fabric, precut for quilting projects. A fat quarter will make quite a few flowers, so the next time you're at the fabric store, try raiding the fat quarters for some new Kanzashi fabrics.

Other Fabric Possibilities. Once you've mastered the basics with cotton, then by all means play around with other fabrics in your stash. A T-shirt knit will yield a softer-looking flower. Linen will yield a very crisp-looking bloom. And imagine how a rich jacquard would look, or bark cloth, or burlap! Once you get the hang of it, you may even want to try your hand at that silk.

You may find that some fabrics work well only for certain sizes or types of flower—a flower made of thick wool fabric, for example, would be nearly impossible to make in any size smaller than three inches. And certain fabrics might need a little tweaking in order to be Kanzashi-ready. That wool I just mentioned? You might want to put a little Fray Check around the edges (a miracle substance that prevents fabric from fraying). Or, if you're working with a thin, delicate silk and finding it challenging to fold, you can always iron some lightweight, fusible interfacing to the back. When I'm playing around with a new fabric, I start by making a

Sometimes a bold print just doesn't look as nice folded up into a Kanzashi flower. Subtler prints tend to be more compatible with lots of folds.

basic three-inch flower, noting what challenges come up during the process and making adjustments from there.

A Note on Prints. If you're a fabric junkie like me, then you probably have a nice stash of

beautiful printed textiles. Are they all good for Kanzashi projects? Well, that will depend. When you make a Kanzashi petal, you fold a square of fabric several times. These folds often obscure the pattern on the fabric. So big, splashy patterns aren't usually the best choice for Kanzashi. Take a look at the photo on the previous page—I adore that blue and cream floral, but when folded into a flower, it looks more like camouflage! Save those splashy prints for other projects and try making your Kanzashi with smaller, more subtle prints instead. Designs made of several tones of the same color work especially well. You can still discern the pattern after the fabric is folded, and it adds a pleasing texture to your finished flowers.

GLUE

You'll need several different kinds of glue to complete the projects in this book, and each one does a different job.

Hot Glue Gun. Love it or hate it, a hot glue gun is an invaluable tool for making the nontraditional Kanzashi in this book. I use hot glue to attach a fabric circle to the back of my finished flower; this glue sets very quickly, so it gives the flower instant stability. Hot glue will bond fabric to fabric quite well, but I don't recommend it for gluing embellishments to flowers. Once hot glue dries, nonporous things such as buttons can pop right off. For gluing centers to your flowers, you'll need embellishment glue.

I recommend using a low-temp hot glue gun, which, as the name implies, is a little less hot than its high-temp cousin.

However, don't be fooled—a low-temp glue gun can still burn you! Be careful to keep your fingers away from the glue and the metal parts of your glue gun, and never leave your glue gun unattended.

Embellishment Glue. For attaching a button center to your flower, or adding stamens, you'll want to use glue that's designed to attach embellishments to fabric. Embellishment glue is designed to bond a nonporous surface to a porous one, so I also use it when I need to attach a flower to a hair clip or an earring finding. I've used brands such as Gem-Tac, Aleene's Jewel-It, and Jewel-Bond successfully.

Fabric Glue. An all-purpose craft glue, such as Aleene's Tacky Glue or Beacon's Fabri-Tac, is great for bonding two porous surfaces together, such as fabric to fabric. I use it to attach flowers to fabric projects like tote bags. I like to put a small dot of glue on the center back of a flower and then press it into place. Once the glue dries, I stitch down the edges of the petals. That initial gluing keeps the flower from moving around as I'm sewing. Why would I not use hot glue for this step? Hot glue is thick, so it can raise the flower slightly above the surface to which I'm gluing it. Fabric glue is thinner, and therefore allows the flower to sit flat on the surface.

E6000. I'm a great fan of this glue, although admittedly, it's somewhat toxic. E6000 is a one-part epoxy, designed to bond both porous and nonporous objects together permanently. I use it when I need to bond things that will be handled a lot—like the Bloomin' Cute Drawer Knobs on page 128. Use E6000 in a well-ventilated space, and follow the package directions for drying time and proper cleanup.

Just a note on "superglues" here: You might think they're a good substitute for E6000, but they aren't. Superglues (cyanoacrylate, sold under various brand names, including Super Glue and Krazy Glue) are very brittle when they dry, so over time, a project adhered with them has a good chance of breaking apart. In contrast, E6000 makes a flexible bond and will stand up to lots of wear.

FINISHING TOUCHES

No Kanzashi flower would be complete without a decorative center element. Here are some possibilities.

Buttons. I use all kinds of buttons on my flowers. Shank buttons (the kind with the little hook on the back that you sew through) are lovely, and you can find so many interesting ones at your local craft store or on eBay. Look for a button that's large enough to completely cover any raw edges of fabric in the center of your flower. If I want the button center to match the flower, then I'll make a covered button, like the one I've used on the Elegant Floral Gift Topper on page 110. Many fabric stores carry simple covered-button kits in a variety of sizes.

Sew-through buttons (the kind with a flat back and holes) also make cute flower centers. Sometimes I glue them on as is, while other times I add a dash of color to them by sewing up the holes. It's easy: Just thread up a needle with bright thread, doubled, with no knot at the end. Bring the needle up through the first hole in your button, leaving a six-inch tail of thread behind the button. Then stitch back and forth through the button holes a few times. Tie the two ends of the thread together at the back and voilà! A button that looks sewn on, but isn't.

Beads. For very small flowers, you might try using decorative beads as your centers. The bead should be large enough to cover all raw fabric edges in the center of the flower. It will be taller than a button, but will lend the flower its own unique style. To attach a bead, simply glue it in place, making sure the holes in the bead face to the sides. (You can see some bead centers in action on the following page as well as in the Kanzashi Bouquet project on page 100.)

Stamens. Faux pearl-head stamens add a gorgeous touch to Kanzashi, and come in lots of pretty colors. You can sometimes locate them in the wedding section of your craft store, or check the Resources section to find them online (see page 142). You can tuck them under a button center, or poke a bundle of them into the middle hole of a flower. I've used them in the Kanzashi Bouquet project on page 100, and also in the Flowers-in-Your-Hair Clips on page 54. See the instructions for those projects to find out more about attaching stamens.

Brooches and Earrings. No, I'm not kidding! Raid your jewelry box or local thrift store for sparkly brooches and post-style earrings, which make very glamorous flower centers. Before you can glue them to a Kanzashi, you may need to use a pair of wire cutters to remove the pin or post.

Felt. If you like, you can cut a circle from some wool or acrylic felt and use that for a center. You can also embellish the felt by stitching on some beads or sequins, or drawing on it with puff paints (decorative kids' fabric paints).

CORE TECHNIQUES

If you've ever tried your hand at origami (the Japanese art of paper-folding), then the three petal folds we will learn in this chapter will feel very familiar to you. If you haven't, don't worry—they're very easy to pick up with practice. Petal-folding is rather meditative, and it's fun to watch your pile of finished petals grow as you dream up ways to combine them into pretty flowers. Assembling the flower is really the only tricky part of the Kanzashi-making process, but with a little practice (and the helpful tips starting on page 28), you'll be turning out gardens of flowers in no time.

CUTTING SQUARES

All the Kanzashi petals in this book begin with squares of fabric. You don't need any fancy equipment to cut them, just a good pair of scissors and a square template. I like to keep a bag of template squares that I've cut from cardstock in various sizes (1–4^1/$_2$"). That way I'm always ready to cut any size of fabric squares I need.

Since most flowers require only a handful of petals, I usually cut my squares by holding the cardstock template to the fabric and cutting along the edges. You can also place the template on the fabric and trace the edges with a pencil before cutting. If you have a rotary cutter, you can certainly use that to cut your squares, but since I'm usually cutting so few at a time, I don't bother. (For a project like the Bloomin' Cute Drawer Knobs on page 128, however, where you need to create many flowers at once, it does make sense to use a rotary cutter.)

PERFECT SQUARES?

Good news: Kanzashi folds are very forgiving. If your squares aren't quite perfect, or the corners don't quite match up in folding, it will never show up in the finished flower. Take my word for it!

TO PRESS OR NOT TO PRESS?

As you fold your way through the petal designs in this book, you may be tempted to iron each fold as you make it. You certainly can, but I tend to think it's not necessary. In fact, for the Round petal style, too much pressing can even ruin the petal shape. I always press the first fold of any petal—the one where you fold the square in half diagonally. After that, I simply press each fold in place with my fingers, so this is how I've recommended you do it in all the project instructions. You may want to make a few petals with all their folds pressed, however, just to see how that looks.

You can press your petal folds with an ordinary household iron, but if you like to make miniature flowers, I recommend investing in an appliqué iron. These wand-style irons, which are available at quilting stores, have a compact, hot surface for pressing, so they can help you press tiny folds without burning your fingers.

PINNING IT DOWN

As you finish folding each petal, you'll stick a pin through the base to hold its shape until you're ready to make a flower. I like to use long, pearl-headed pins for this step—and they should be sharp! Each Kanzashi petal will have many layers of fabric, so the sharper the pin, the more easily it will pass through.

~~~~~~~~~~~~~~~~

You don't need any fancy equipment to cut fabric squares for Kanzashi—just a cardstock template and scissors.

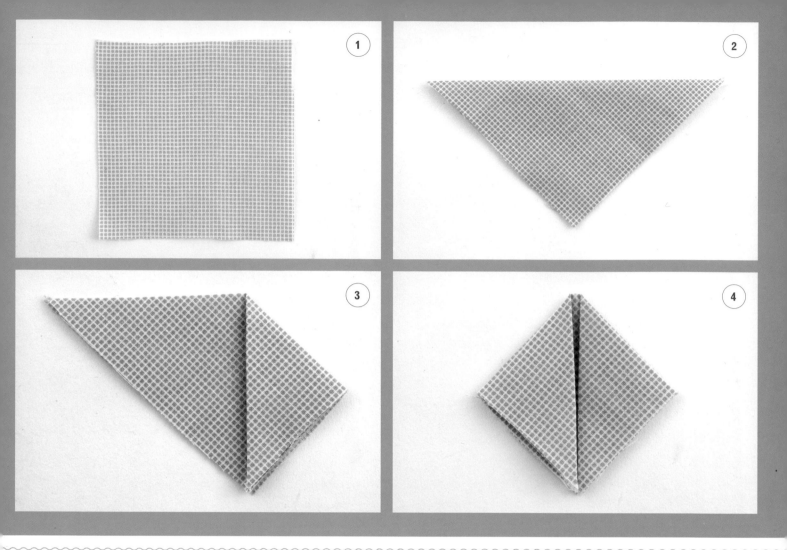

BASIC INSTRUCTIONS: ROUND KANZASHI PETAL

The Round petal has a lovely teardrop shape that lends itself well to all kinds of flower designs. It is the simplest petal design in the book, so it's also easy to make in large and small sizes, and you can craft it with thicker materials such as leather and vinyl. When you mix and match this petal design with the Pointed or Pleated petals, you can create an endless array of flowers.

In this tutorial, I've pressed the fabric with an iron after nearly every fold to make for an extra-sharp-looking petal. If you make this petal using finger-pressing instead, as the instructions suggest, then you'll end up with a slightly softer look.

1. Begin with a square of fabric. If you're just learning this craft, I recommend using a square that is 3" or larger.

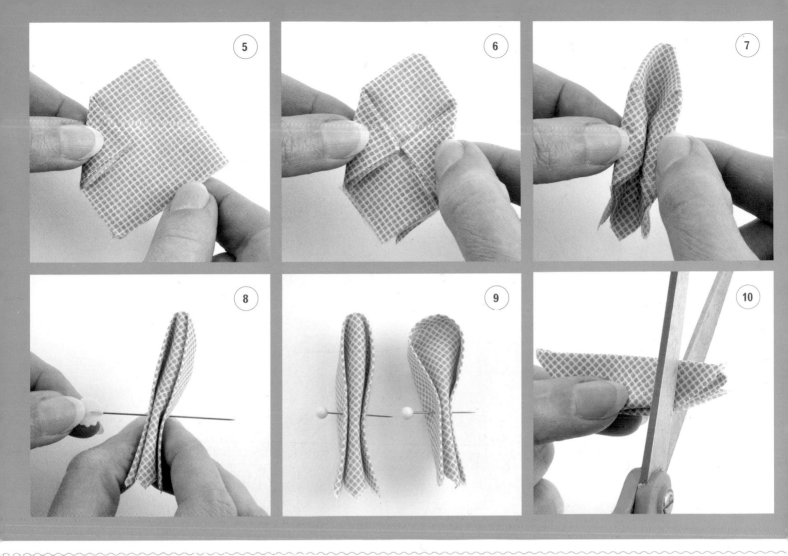

2. Fold this square in half diagonally, with the right side of the fabric facing out. Press this fold with an iron.

3. Take the right-hand corner, and fold it down to meet the bottom corner. Press the fold with your fingers.

4. Do the same thing with the left-hand corner. Press the fold with your fingers.

5. Now flip over the whole piece so you're looking at the back. Take the left-hand corner and fold it in to meet the center. Press the fold with your fingers.

6. Repeat with the right-hand corner. Press the fold with your fingers. The two corners should meet in the center but not overlap.

7. Fold the whole piece in half, toward you, capturing those two corners inside the fold. This is now the back of your petal.

8. Turn the petal over, and the front will look like this. Stick a pin through the bottom of the petal. This is how you hold your petal's shape until you're ready to assemble it into a flower.

9. This petal can be used in two different ways: If you open the top of the petal a little with your thumb and forefinger, it will round out into a teardrop shape. If you pinch together the tip of the petal, it becomes long and narrow.

10. When you're ready to incorporate this petal into a Kanzashi flower, you'll need to trim the base, as shown. Cut straight across the petal, starting at the lowest point of the diagonal raw edge.

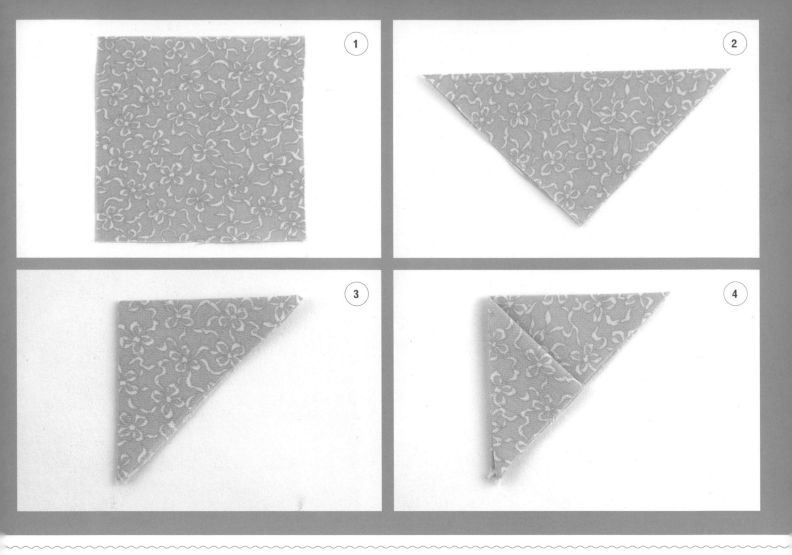

BASIC INSTRUCTIONS: POINTED KANZASHI PETAL

The Pointed petal is the sturdiest of the three petal formation styles in this book. I like to use it in projects that will end up being handled a lot. This petal is taller at the center than at the tip, so the flowers you make with it will have a slightly domed shape. You can also combine this petal design with Round or Pleated petals.

1. Begin with a square of fabric. If you're just learning this craft, I recommend using a square that is 3" or larger.

2. Fold this square in half diagonally, with the right side of the fabric facing out. Press this fold with an iron.

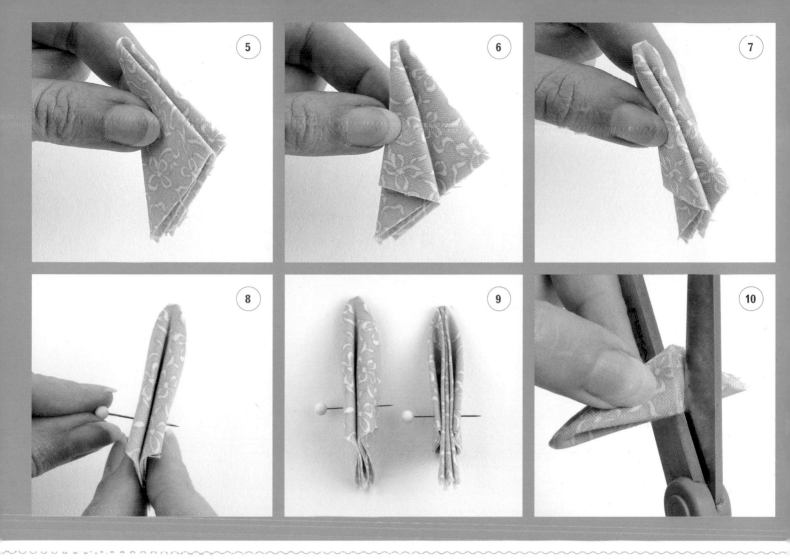

3. Fold the resulting triangle in half crosswise. Press this fold with your fingers.

4. Place this triangle so that you can see two folds on the top side and one fold on the left side. Now take the top layer of the right-hand corner and fold it toward you until it meets the bottom corner, as shown. Press this fold with your fingers.

5. Flip over the petal and repeat Step 4 on the other side. Press this fold with your fingers. Now the two sides of the petal should match.

6. Hold the resulting triangle so that you can see three folds on the left side and two folds on the right. Take the top layer of the right-hand side and fold it toward you so it meets the left side, as shown. Press this fold with your fingers.

7. Flip over the petal and repeat Step 6 on the other side. Press this fold with your fingers. Now the two sides of the petal should match again.

8. Put a pin through the base of the petal to secure it.

9. This petal has two different aspects: Use the simpler side facing up, or flip it over for a more elaborate appearance.

10. When you're ready to incorporate this petal into a Kanzashi flower, you'll need to trim off the base, as shown. Cut right along the bottom edge of the outermost fold.

BASIC INSTRUCTIONS: PLEATED KANZASHI PETAL

This petal design was born when I was teaching a Kanzashi class and one of my students misunderstood my directions for making a Pointed petal. I'm so glad she did—I love the look of this petal! The Pleated petal is probably the most challenging to learn to fold, so I recommend practicing the Round and Pointed styles a little before you attempt this one.

1. Begin with a square of fabric. If you're just learning this craft, I recommend using a square that is 3" or larger.

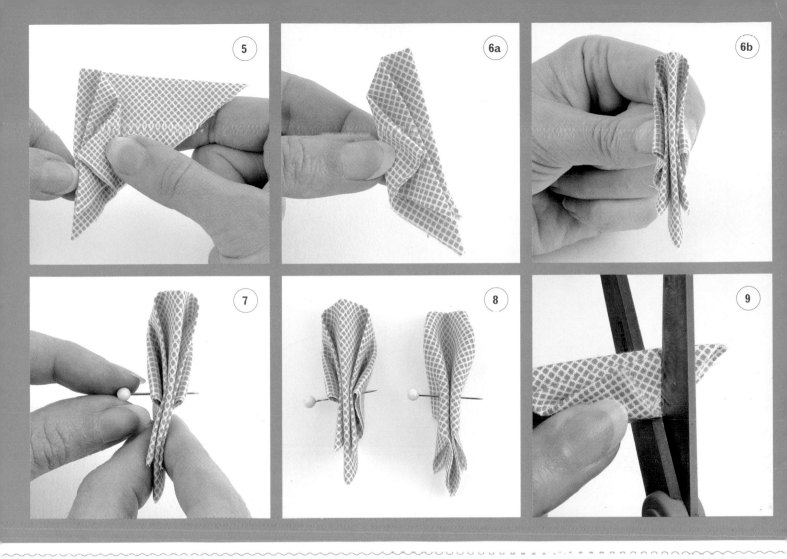

2. Fold this square in half diagonally, with the right side of the fabric facing out. Press this fold with an iron.

3. Fold the resulting triangle in half crosswise. Press this fold with your fingers.

4. Place this triangle so that you can see two folds on the top side and one fold on the left side. Now take the top layer of the right-hand corner and fold it toward you. Bring this corner to about 1/4" above the bottom corner, as shown. Press this fold with your fingers.

5. Take the new top layer of the right-hand corner and fold it toward you as well. Bring this corner to about 1/2" above the bottom corner, as shown. Press this fold with your fingers.

6a. Turn the petal over and repeat Steps 4 and 5. **b.** Take a look at this view of the front of the petal. See how I've folded the points to match the same places on both sides? This gives your petal a balanced shape.

7. Put a pin through the base of the petal to secure it.

8. Consider that you can use this petal two different ways: With the pleated side facing up, you have a nice ruffled look. Or, flip it over for a simpler, blunt edge.

9. When you're ready to incorporate this petal into a Kanzashi flower, you'll need to trim off the base, as shown. Cut straight across the petal at the bottom of the outermost fold.

ASSEMBLING A KANZASHI FLOWER

The instructions in the next section will take you step by step through the process of assembling your finished petals into a Kanzashi flower. But before we get there, here are a few important things to know.

How to Size a Flower. Interestingly, the size of fabric square you use to fold each petal will be the same size as your finished flower. So if you make your petals from three-inch squares, the finished flower will be about three inches in diameter. Remember that bag of variously sized cardstock templates I told you about in the last section? Well, it also comes in handy when trying to decide what size flower to make for a tote bag or scarf. You can hold the various squares up to the templates to help visualize how a flower that size would look.

How Many Petals? You can make Kanzashi with any number of petals you like, but in general, the larger your flower, the more petals you are likely to need. A three-and-a-half-inch flower with only five petals, for example, will end up with too much space between each petal, and as a result be somewhat floppy. More petals provide more stability, especially with larger flowers. Conversely, smaller flowers work well with fewer petals. A two-inch flower looks lovely with six petals, but ten petals would be quite crowded. I find myself coming back again and again to eight-petal and ten-petal flowers. They work well in a variety of sizes, and they offer many design possibilities, especially if you're mixing fabric or petal styles. Which brings me to my next point.

Your finished flower will be the same size as the squares you used to fold the petals.

Other Design Options. Ah, here's the fun part! When you're designing a flower, you have lots of decisions to make: How many petals will you use? What size will they be? Which fabrics should you choose? And then you also have all these design options:

Making all your petals the same color.

Making your petals in multiple colors.

Having all your petals be the same style.

Mixing several petal styles.

Having all your petals be the same size.

Combining two or three different-sized petals.

For each project in this book, I'll make suggestions as to the best petal sizes and styles, and the optimal number of petals. But feel free to experiment! There are no hard-and-fast rules. I think you'll find that designing Kanzashi becomes pretty addictive.

Backing It Up. For the most part, the last step in making any Kanzashi flower is to cut a circle of fabric and glue it to the back of the flower. We do this for two reasons: first, to cover up the raw edges of fabric at the center back of the flower;

and second, to help stabilize the flower. When you glue fabric over the backs of the petals, it fixes them in place so your flower doesn't droop or lose its shape. As my backing, I usually like to use a circle of the same fabric from which I made the flower, unless I'm making a project where the back of my flower will see a lot of wear, such as the Flower Power Pendant on page 40. In those cases, I use a circle of wool felt instead. If you're not comfortable cutting circles freehand, you can use a circle template and trace it onto the fabric with a pencil before cutting.

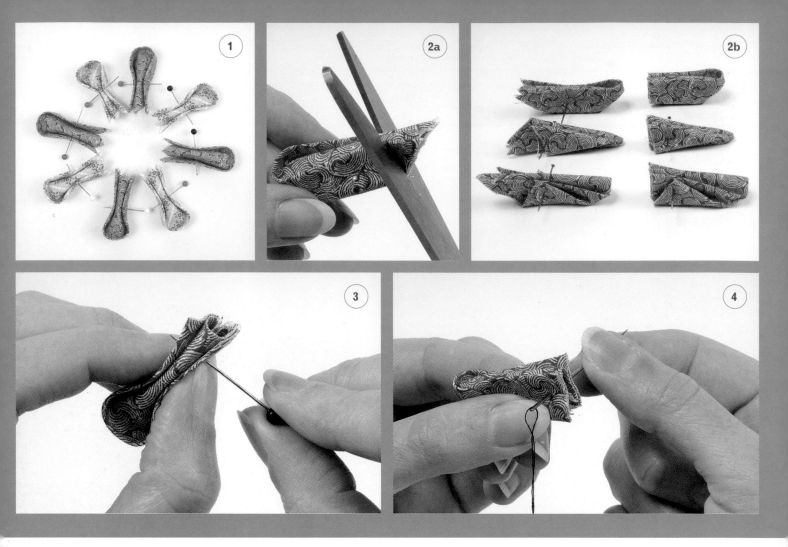

BASIC FLOWER ASSEMBLY

This is a simple method for building a flower from a group of petals. It is best used with petals you've folded from fabric; if you're working with vinyl or leather petals, as in the Happiest Belt Buckle Ever on page 76, then use the glue assembly method detailed in that project.

First decide how many petals you'd like your flower to have, and in what styles and colors. Fold the number of petals you need, using the Basic Instructions outlined in the previous section. In addition to the fabric you chose for your flowers, cardstock squares, and straight pins used to form the petals, you will also need to assemble these materials:

- A long, sharp sewing needle. I love crewel embroidery needles because they have a large eye and are easy to thread.
- Strong all-purpose thread in any color (it will be hidden inside the flower, so it doesn't have to match the fabrics, but it should coordinate with them).
- Sharp scissors
- An extra scrap of fabric to cover the back of your flower
- Low-temperature glue gun
- Circle template and pencil (optional)
- Embellishment for the center of your flower: a nice button or bead, or some faux floral stamens

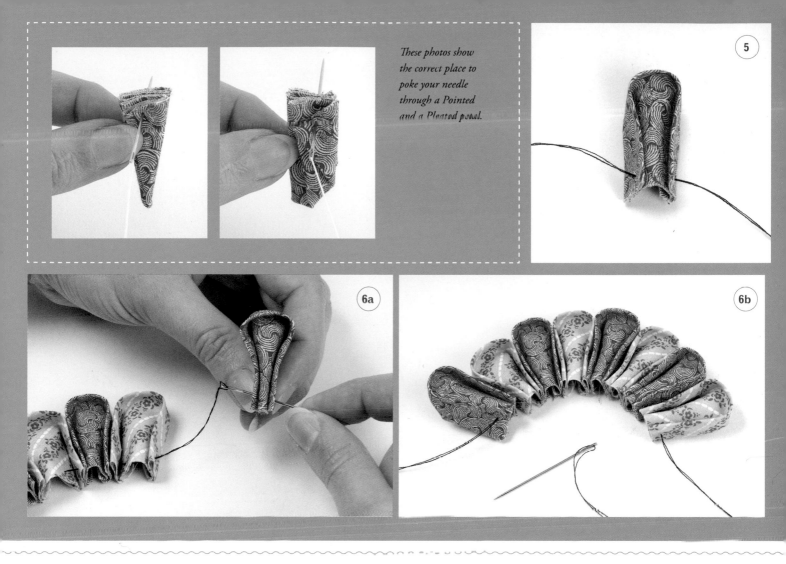

These photos show the correct place to poke your needle through a Pointed and a Pleated petal.

1. If you're practicing this assembly technique for the first time, I recommend starting with eight petals of the same size and style. As you get more comfortable with the technique, you can try mixing petal designs and sizes, and using different numbers of petals. Take a moment to lay your petals out in front of you, in the order they will appear in your finished flower.

2a and 2b. Trim off the end of each petal, as described in the Basic Instructions in the previous section. Remember, each petal style is trimmed a little differently; the second image gives you a refresher course in how the ends should look.

3. Thread your needle with doubled thread, but don't tie a knot. Pick up the first petal, making sure you're pinching the base together firmly so it won't come unfolded. Then remove its pin.

4. Keeping a good hold on that petal, poke the needle through the base. The needle should be about 1/8" away from the raw edge of the petal and centered across its width, as shown in the two photos above left.

5. Pull the thread through the petal, leaving about a 4" tail hanging loose. You can let go of your petal at this point. It may unfold a little, but the thread will keep it from coming apart. When you add more petals and group them together, they will begin to push each other back into shape.

6a and 6b. Repeat Steps 2–5 with each of the remaining petals, until they are all strung side-by-side on the thread, like beads. Be very careful as you string the petals to make sure they are all facing the same way and in the order you want. (If you do accidentally string one on backwards, don't worry! See the Fixes section on page 34.)

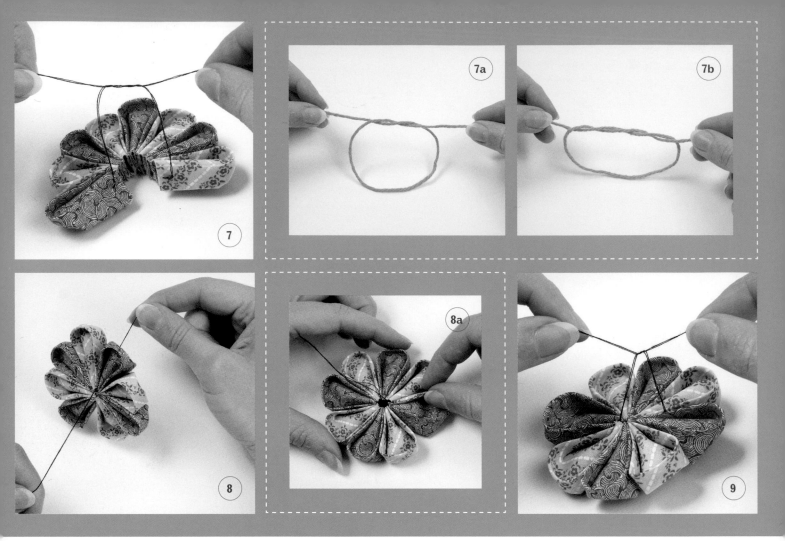

7. Cut the leading end of the thread to remove the needle. Tie the two ends of the thread in a surgeon's knot.

7a and 7b. If you're not familiar with a surgeon's knot, let's take a closer look. It begins with the simple overhand knot you usually tie when you begin to tie your shoe, as shown in **a**. Then you pass the thread through the middle a second time, as shown in **b**.

8. Taking one end of the thread in each hand, pull the surgeon's knot to tighten it (but not too tight—see Step 9). As it tightens, your petals will form a circle.

8a. You may need to let go of the ends of the thread for a moment, adjust the position of the petals a little, and then retighten the knot. In fact, you may need to straighten the petals and retighten the knot a few times before your flower forms a nice circle. This is the trickiest part of the process, so take your time. (If your flower is refusing to form a proper circle, see the Fixes section on page 34.)

One helpful tip: See how I'm pulling the thread ends perpendicular to the flower? That helps it take shape more easily.

9. Be careful not to pull the knot too tight! Your flower should have a small hole in the center, with the petals arranged comfortably around it, as shown here. The petals should fit snugly; if they're too loose, then tighten your knot a little. When the flower petals are arranged the way you desire, tie a second knot in the thread to anchor the flower in place.

10. Pull the loose ends of the thread toward the center of the flower and cut them close, as shown. The tiny ends of the thread will disappear inside the flower.

11a and 11b. Place your flower on a work surface so that the underside is facing up. Sometimes you'll see that a petal fold or two has popped out of place while you assembled the flower. Not to worry—you can fix these now.

12a and 12b. To secure your flower, cut a small circle of fabric to glue to the back. Your circle should be large enough to fully cover any exposed raw edges of fabric in your flower's center. Use a circle template to trace a circle, or simply cut one freehand. Attach the circle to the back of your flower with hot glue.

13. Turn over the flower so the front side faces up. Then use embellishment glue to attach something cute to the center. *Voilà!*

FIXES: WHAT TO DO IF SOMETHING GOES WRONG

You may need to sacrifice a few flowers before you master this assembly technique. Here are some common goofs that might occur while you're learning the craft. If they do, don't panic! Take a deep breath and try one of these quick fixes.

Oops! I Strung a Petal Backwards! Don't worry, this happens from time to time. See that petal, second to the right, below? If the errant petal is near the end of the thread, then you can just slip the few petals before it off the string, making sure to replace a pin in each one as you remove it from the thread (so your petal doesn't lose its folds). Then remove the backward petal and place a pin in it. Slide the remaining petals farther down the thread, and then restring the ones you just removed, making sure they all face in the same direction.

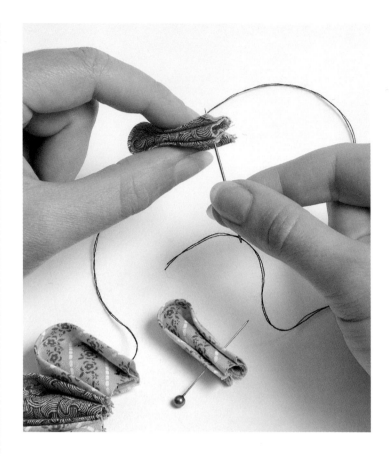

Now, if your backward petal is closer to the needle end of the thread, you don't have to unstring your whole flower. Instead, cut the thread close to the needle in order to liberate the petal; then pull off and repin as many petals as you need to in order to remove the backwards one. Take the leading end of the thread, and rethread the two strands through your needle together. Proceed with restringing the petals. This same fix also works if you accidentally string your petals in the wrong order.

My Flower Won't Make a Circle. As I mentioned in Step 8a on page 32, pulling the knot in the thread to form a circular flower is a little tricky. If your flower is stubbornly refusing to form a proper circle, the petals on either side of the knot are usually the culprits.

When you tighten the knot in the thread, the two petals on either side of it sometimes wind up being end-to-end, not side-by-side. If this happens, let go of the thread for a moment. Take the two petals that are closest to the knot and give them a little twist with your fingers so that they lay side-by-side, as shown. Then try tightening the thread again.

My Flower Won't Hold Together—the Petals Are Flopping Around. This probably means that you didn't tie the thread tightly enough. If you've already double-knotted it and cut off the ends, don't worry. You can cheat a little and save yourself the trouble of restringing the petals. Carefully place your flower face down on a work surface. Cut a slightly larger circle of fabric than is called for in the Basic Flower Assembly Instructions—one that covers the entire back center of the flower.

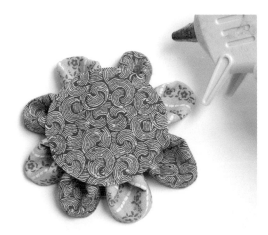

With your flower face down, carefully push and prod the petals into position, arranging them until they are equally spaced around the center. If any of your petals have folds of fabric coming loose, tuck them back into place. When you have the flower looking nice, apply plenty of hot glue to the back and press the fabric circle gently over the glue. This should give your flower plenty of stability.

When I Cut the Thread, the Whole Flower Came Apart! Oops! This can happen. When you trim the loose ends of the thread in Step 10 on page 33, don't cut them too close. If you do accidentally cut the thread that holds your flower together, you can always pull off all the petals, repin them, and then start again with a new thread.

~~~~~~~~~~~~~~~~~~~~~~~

TWO SPECIAL TECHNIQUES

~~~~~~~~~~~~~~~~~~~~~~~

The projects in this book deal with some simple sewing and jewelry-making techniques. Although there is much to learn about each of these subjects, to make the projects, you can get by with these two easy techniques.

WHIPSTITCH
This user-friendly hand-sewing method securely joins two or more layers of fabric. To begin,

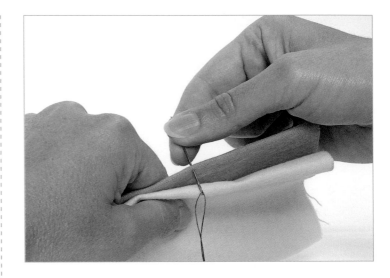

thread a sewing needle with single thread and tie a knot at the longer end.

You'll want to hide this knot as you begin stitching, so for the very first stitch, pass your needle through only the topmost layer of fabric, as shown above. When you pull the thread through, the knot will then be hidden in between the two layers, out of sight.

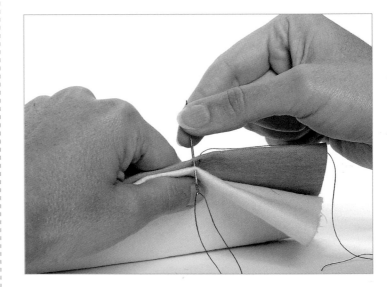

From there, pass the needle up through both layers, as shown at bottom left, catching just a little of each fabric in the needle. Pull that stitch through, and then repeat it numerous times. The main secret to the whipstitch is that you always pass the needle through the fabric in the same direction, as shown below.

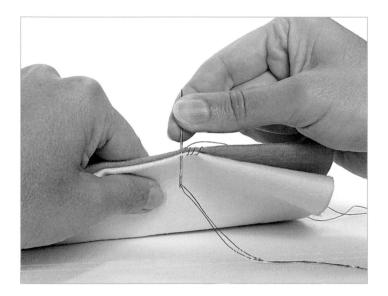

OPENING AND CLOSING A JUMP RING

Jump rings are those crucial little round connectors that join and link jewelry components. They may seem tricky to work with but are actually quite simple, as long as you handle them properly.

The best way to open a jump ring is to twist it open, as shown at top right. I usually grip one side of the ring in my fingers and the other side with a pair of needle-nose pliers. If you find this challenging, try holding each side of the ring with a separate pair of pliers.

Never open a jump ring by pulling the ends apart: That will only pull the ring out of shape and make it impossible to close.

To close a jump ring, simply push the ends back together and mash them flat at the closure with the pliers, as shown at bottom. You want to make sure there is no gap in the ring once it's closed. If your ring is stubbornly holding a little gap, you can always use a toothpick to apply a tiny dot of superglue there; just keep the jump ring away from the other parts of your project until the superglue dries.

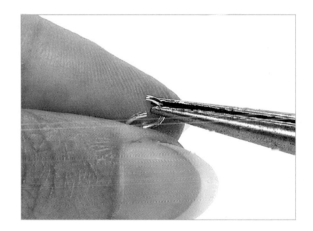

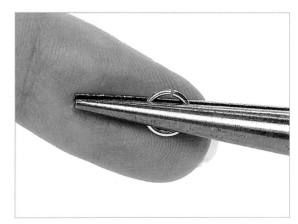

Projects to Wear

Now, let's try to answer that perennial question: "What can you do with these flowers?" These projects show you lots of ways you can adorn yourself (or your favorite people) with Kanzashi. There are projects here for all seasons: Adorn your sandals with some Kanzashi shoe clips in the spring (page 59) and cozy up all winter with a Fuzzy-Flower Scarf (page 64). If you like your accessories on the delicate side, try some Tiny Blossom Earrings (page 44); but if you're of a bolder persuasion, you'll love the Happiest Belt Buckle Ever (page 76). Let's add some flower power to your wardrobe!

Flower Power Pendant

If you hoard precious little scraps of fabric, this project just might be the perfect way to use them. I love how flexible these pendants are—depending on the fabrics you use, they can be a fun complement to jeans or an elegant addition to your prettiest dress. You can also play around with the size, making your pendant big and dramatic or small and delicate.

Before You Begin

- An eye pin is a thin metal pin with a loop at one end. You can find eye pins in the jewelry-making section of your craft store.

- If you find it challenging to work with this size of fabric squares, you might try making your pendant larger, or incorporating some of the techniques for working with small Kanzashi in the Tiny Blossom Earrings project on Page 44.

Skill Level
Beginner
(Practice making a few flowers first.)

Best Petal Styles
Round, Pointed, Pleated

Best Number of Petals
6–10

Best Square Size
1³/₄"

Glues Needed
Hot glue, embellishment glue

Additional Supplies Needed
- Scrap of wool felt
- One 24-gauge eye pin, at least 1" long
- One 8-mm jump ring
- Neck wire or chain necklace
- Sharp scissors
- Wire cutters
- Needle-nose pliers

MAKING A PENDANT

1. Make a flower using the Basic Instructions in Chapter 2. Cut a 1¼" circle of felt for the back of your flower, but don't glue it on yet. Using wire cutters, trim the eye pin to approximately the length shown here.

2. Apply a ring of embellishment glue to the center back of the flower. Position the eye pin on the glue, as shown, making sure that the eye sits behind the topmost petal of the flower.

3. Press the felt circle over the glue. Allow the glue to dry completely.

4. Use needle-nose pliers to open the jump ring, as shown. Thread it through the eye pin and close it. String your pendant onto the neck wire or chain.

This pendant design can easily be adapted to create a cute charm or dangle, like the one on this beaded bracelet. Or, try making a necklace that has several Kanzashi pendants dangling from it.

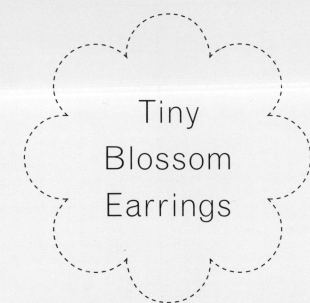

Tiny
Blossom
Earrings

Whenever I teach classes in Kanzashi-making, the first thing many of my students do is attempt to see how small they can make their flowers. I think the all-time record holder was able to do it with half-inch squares! We're not going to be quite so ambitious here, but we are going to learn some ways to make miniature flowers. If you're new to Kanzashi, you might want to practice making some larger flowers before you tackle this project.

Before You Begin

- The Round petal is generally your best bet for flowers this small, because it's the simplest to fold. The Pointed and Pleated petals would definitely take lots of practice at this size.
- You'll need to start with very thin cotton fabric. Bulkier fabrics, such as quilting cottons, just won't hold these tiny folds.
- To make a miniature flower, we'll use the Basic Instructions in Chapter 2, with a few small modifications.
- Fray Check is a clear liquid that you apply to the cut edge of fabric to keep it from unraveling. You can usually find it in fabric stores.
- When you make flowers this small, you may find it easier to use an appliqué iron to press the folds in your fabric. This type of iron has a tiny heated surface, which creases fabric neatly without the danger of burning fingers. These are available in craft or quilting store.

Skill Level
Advanced

Best Petal Styles
Round

Best Number of Petals
6

Best Square Size
1"

Glues Needed
Hot glue, embellishment glue

Additional Supplies Needed
- Fray Check sealant
- Thin, small-eyed sewing needle, such as a quilting needle
- One set of post-earring findings with rubber or metal ear nut backs
- Sharp scissors
- Appliqué iron (optional)
- Quilting pins (optional)
- Tweezers (optional)

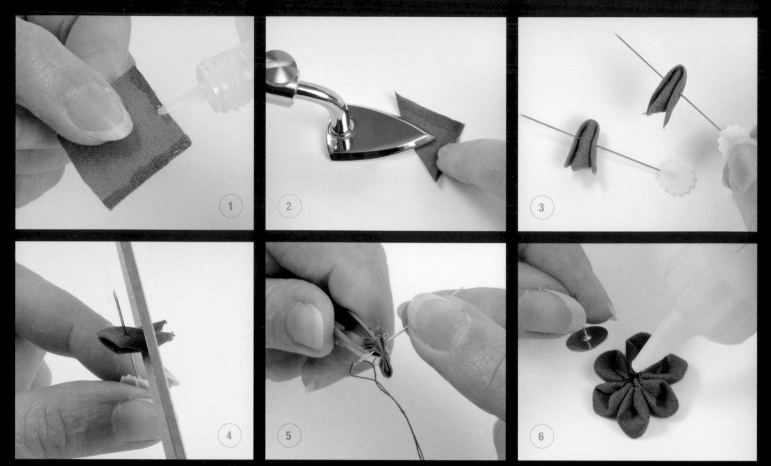

MAKING TINY FLOWERS

1. After cutting out your six fabric squares, treat their edges with Fray Check and allow them to dry. When you're working in these small dimensions, frayed edges and stray threads can really get in the way.

2. Pressing the first fold is essential for tiny flowers (I'm using an appliqué iron here). Finger-pressing will be sufficient for all the folds after this.

3. As you finish folding each petal, pin it as usual. For petals this small, I prefer to use quilting pins, which are very long, thin, and sharp. They'll pass through the layers of fabric easily and provide a nice long "handle" for holding the petal. Place those pins high up on the petal, as shown.

4. Trim the base off each petal according to the Basic Instructions in Chapter 2. When you place the pin high on

the petal as recommended in Step 3, you'll find it much easier to maneuver your scissors into position.

5. Assemble the flower according to the instructions in Chapter 2. String together the petals as usual, but use a small, thin needle, which will pass more easily through the layers of fabric. You may also find it easier to hold each petal with a pair of tweezers, as shown, when you pass the needle through.

MAKING EARRINGS

6. Using embellishment glue, attach a tiny button or bead to the center of each flower. Then glue the backs of the flowers to the earring posts. Allow the glue to dry completely. Add a rubber or metal ear nut backing to each earring.

Make an adorable floral ring by gluing your mini-flower to an adjustable ring base. In fact, make a whole handful! Or, if you like these tiny flowers, you can alter many of the projects in this book so they're adorned with lots of little blossoms instead of one large one.

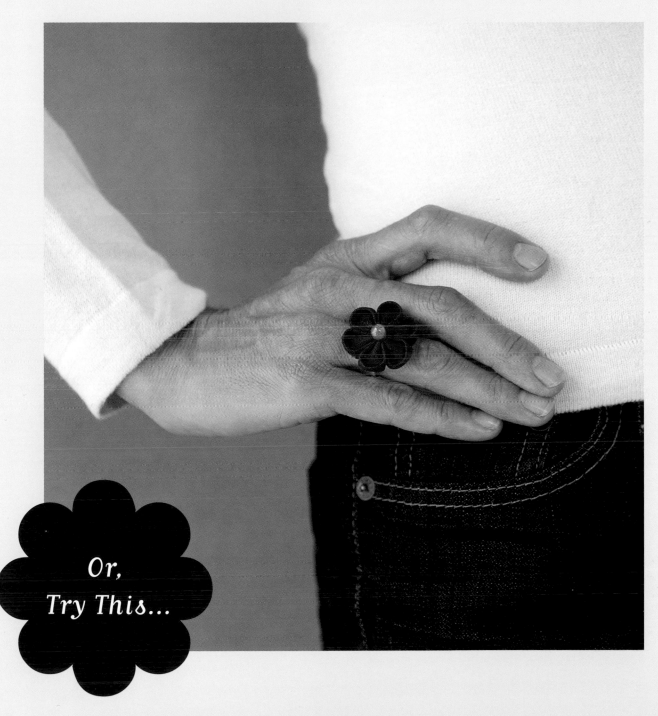

Or,
Try This...

Cheerful Cuff

I love the look of a bright, colorful cuff bracelet. Add a Kanzashi flower, and you have something reminiscent of a prom night wrist corsage, but with a cheekier feel. This is a great simple project for beginning stitchers, and the cuff base makes a wonderful blank canvas to adorn with any fantastic flower you create.

Before You Begin
- All seam allowances in this project are $1/4$".
- Depending on your preference, you can close your bracelet with elastic loops and buttons or with simple Velcro dots.

Skill Level
Beginner

Best Petal Styles
Round, Pointed, Pleated

Best Number of Petals
6–10

Best Square Size
2"

Glues Needed
Hot glue, embellishment glue, fabric glue

Additional Supplies Needed
- Two pieces of coordinating cotton fabric
- Scrap of flannel fabric
- Coordinating thread and sewing needle
- Straight pins
- Measuring tape
- Fabric-marking pen
- Oval elastic cord (available at fabric stores)
- Two coordinating $1/2$" buttons
- Two sets of $1/2$" sew-on Velcro dots, black (optional)
- Sharp scissors
- Chopstick
- Sewing machine
- Hot iron

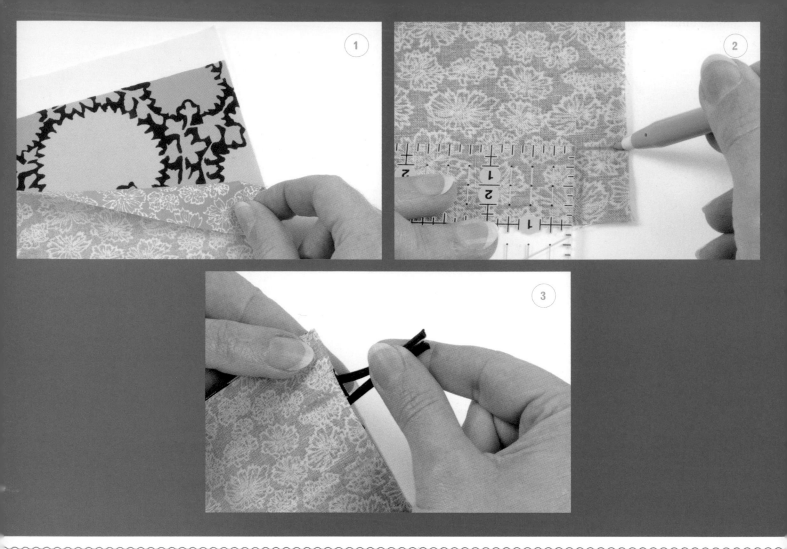

1. Use the measuring tape to measure around your wrist. Make sure the tape is wrapped comfortably and not too tight. Add 2¹/₂" to your wrist measurement and then cut a rectangle from your cotton fabric, matching that measurement in length by 3" in height. (For example, my wrist measures 6¹/₂", so my rectangle is 9 × 3".) Cut matching rectangles from the other cotton fabric and the flannel.

2. Place the right sides of two cotton rectangles together. Then place the flannel rectangle beneath the stacked cotton ones. (It will be hidden between the cotton layers in the finished cuff.) Match all the edges, and pin the three pieces together. Using a fabric-marking pen, draw two marks on one of the 3" edges of the cotton fabric. The marks should be 1" in from either corner, as shown. (If you don't want to use the elastic-and-button closure, you can skip this last step and Step 3.)

3. Cut two 3" pieces of elastic cord. Fold each one in half. Insert them between the two layers of cotton fabric so that the folded end is inside. Place a piece of elastic at each of the marks you made in Step 2. Adjust them so that a ¹/₂" loop of elastic will appear to the left of your seam, inside the fabric. Pin the elastic in place.

4. Sew the three rectangles together, as shown, leaving about a 3" gap in the seam along one of the long edges. When you sew over the elastic loops, backstitch over them so that they're securely attached. After sewing, trim away the seam allowances at the corners. (This will create a more precise point when you turn the corners right-side out.)

5. Use the gap you left in the seam to turn the cuff right-side out, poking a chopstick into each corner to ensure that it's nice and sharp. Use an iron to press the cuff flat, folding under the raw edges of the gap and pressing them down. Topstitch ¼" from all four edges. Topstitch again closer to the four edges.

6. Make a flower, but don't add a center yet. (The flower will alter its shape a little when the cuff is wrapped around your wrist, so we'll put the center on in a later step.) Use a little fabric glue to tack the flower to the center of the cuff, and allow the glue to dry.

7. Attach the tip of each petal to the top layer of the cuff with a tiny whipstitch, as shown.

(continued)

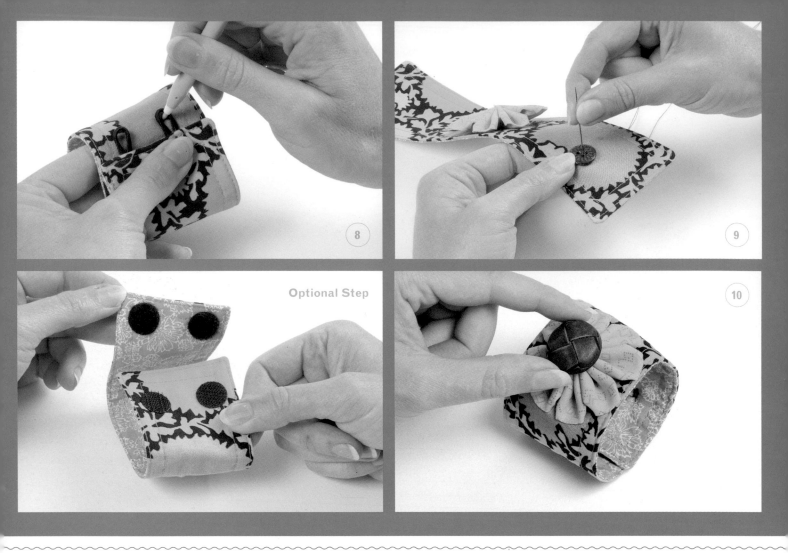

Optional Step

8. Wrap the cuff around your wrist comfortably to determine where the two ends overlap. Remove the cuff, overlap the ends again, and pin them together. The end with the elastic loops should be on top. Use a fabric-marking pen to make a dot inside each of the elastic loops. Unpin and flatten the cuff.

9. Sew a button over each of the dots you marked in Step 8.

Optional Step: If you prefer, you can sew on two sets of Velcro dots to close your bracelet instead of using the buttons and elastic loops.

10. Refasten the buttons or Velcro so that your cuff is circular again. This will reshape the flower a little to the way you want it to be when you attach a center. Use embellishment glue to attach the center and allow it to dry.

You can easily adapt this cuff bracelet pattern to make a dandy cover for a cute needle book holder. Just change the size, fold it in half, and sew in a page or two of felt to hold the needles. They make great gifts for your sewing-buff friends.

Or, Try This...

Flowers-in-Your-Hair Clips

Since traditional Kanzashi are worn as hair ornaments, I had to include some hair clips in this book. There are so many types of blank hairpins, clips, and barrettes available—for those with every hairstyle from short curls to long ponytails. If you can't find them at your local craft store, check online (see Resources). We'll also learn how to attach stamens to embellish your Kanzashi as an elegant alternative to buttons and beads.

Before You Begin

- I've used some faux flower stamens in one of these designs because they make a great-looking center for a very small flower. Stamens are often available in the wedding section of your craft store, or online (see the Resources section).

Skill Level
Beginner

Best Petal Styles
Round, Pointed, Pleated

Best Number of Petals
6–10

Best Square Size
Depending on your blank clip or barrette, anything from $1\frac{1}{2}$" to $3\frac{1}{2}$" fabric squares

Glues Needed
Hot glue, embellishment glue, fabric glue

Additional Supplies Needed
- Pearl-head faux stamens (optional)
- Hair-clip findings of your choice
- Painter's tape
- For the large barrette: wool felt, coordinating thread, needle
- Wire cutters (if you're using stamens)
- Sharp scissors

ADDING A STAMEN CLUSTER

1. If you're working with double-ended stamens, fold them in half, as shown, and gather them into a cluster that's large enough to fit snugly into the center of your flower.

Alternatively, you can buy premade stamen clusters, such as the pink one shown here. With either style, poke the stem ends of the stamens through the center of the flower and pull them through from the back until the cluster of pearl ends sits atop the flower.

2. Use wire cutters to cut all the stems so that they're flush with the back of the flower. When you glue the flower to a hair clip, the glue will ooze into the cut ends of the stamens and hold them in place.

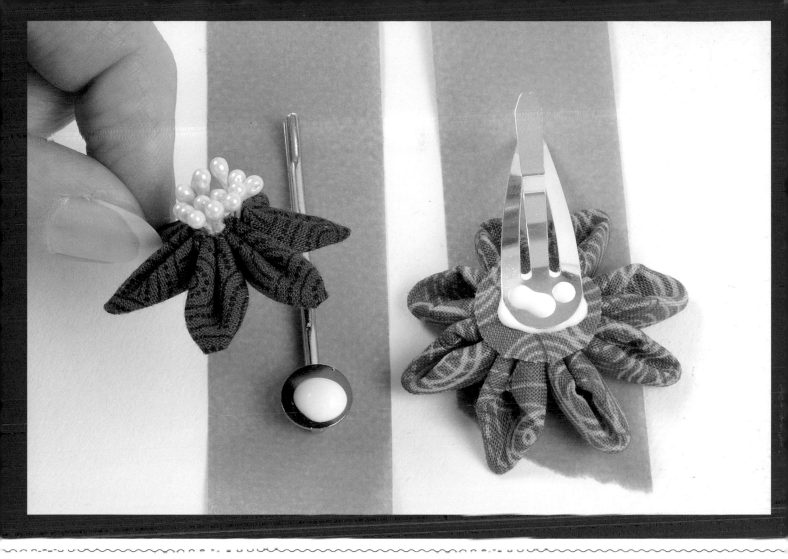

MAKING PINS AND CLIPS

Make a flower for each pin or clip, using the Basic Instructions in Chapter 2. Now you can attach your flower to the pin or clip using embellishment glue. This kind of glue needs about ten minutes to form a bond, and your flower could slip out of place during that time. So, to make sure the flower won't move while it's drying, use a piece of painter's tape (available in hardware stores) to hold the clips in place. Just place a piece of tape, sticky-side up, on your work surface and place the clip on top, as shown. The tape is just sticky enough to keep the clip stationary without damaging its finish. When the glue is fully dry, remove the tape, and your hair ornaments are ready to wear.

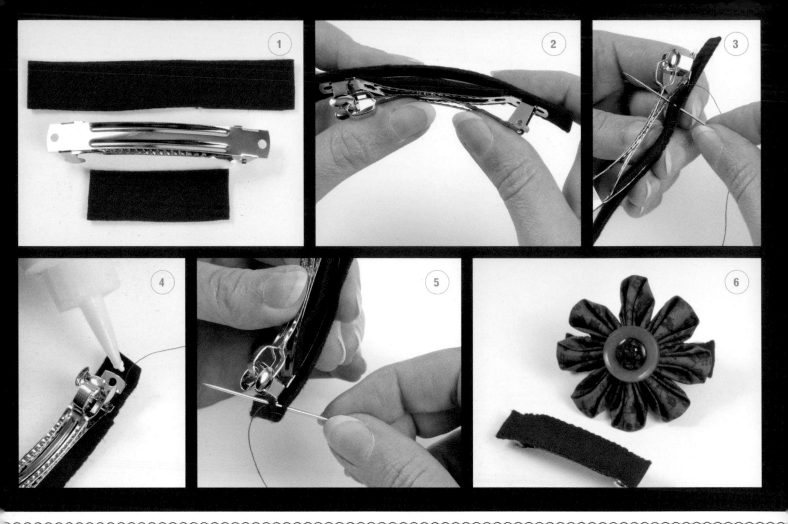

MAKING A BARRETTE

1. These large ponytail barrettes look lovely adorned with a dramatic flower, but I like to first cover up the metal part with felt. So, using your barrette as a gauge, cut two strips of felt ¼" wider than the width of the barrette. One strip should be short enough to tuck into the underside of the barrette, as shown. The other strip should be ½" longer than the length of the barrette.

2. Place these two felt strips over the top and bottom of the barrette, and match up the edges. The short strip should be tucked into the center of the barrette, as shown. Make sure the long strip is centered over the top of the barrette so that the same amount of felt sticks out past each end.

3. Starting in the center, begin stitching the felt strips together around the barrette using a tiny whipstitch.

4. When you reach the end of the barrette, stop sewing for a moment and put a tiny dot of embellishment glue on the end of the felt.

5. Fold the felt over the end of the barrette and stitch the edges securely together. Pass the needle under the felt to move to the other side of the barrette, and continue stitching the other side. Repeat Steps 4 and 5 at the other end of the barrette, and knot the thread once you reach your first stitch.

6. Make a large flower. Using fabric glue, attach your flower to the center of the barrette. (You may find it easiest to open the barrette and lay it flat on some painter's tape before gluing.) Allow the glue to dry completely.

Don't stop with hair clips: Decorate your shoes and hats with Kanzashi shoe clips to really jazz up your wardrobe. Shoe-clip blanks are available at most large craft stores and online.

Stretch &
Bloom
Headband

These cute and comfortable headbands keep your hair out of
your eyes while adding a little flair to your look. I think they'd
look adorable on a little girl—or on a big one! You can adorn
them with as many or as few flowers as you like, and fashion the
flowers in several sizes and styles.

Before You Begin

- This headband uses elastic cord, which is available at fabric stores. Use oval
  cord if you can, because it's so much easier to sew over. If you can't find oval
  cord, try a thinner round cord, or ¹/₄" flat braided elastic. These are all usually
  available in black or white.

Skill Level
Beginner

Best Petal Styles
Round, Pointed, Pleated

Best Number of Petals
6–10

Best Square Size
1¹/₂" to 2¹/₂"

Glue Needed
Hot glue

Additional Supplies Needed
- Oval elastic cord
- Wool felt
- Coordinating thread and
  hand-sewing needle
- Sharp scissors
- Measuring tape
- Sewing machine

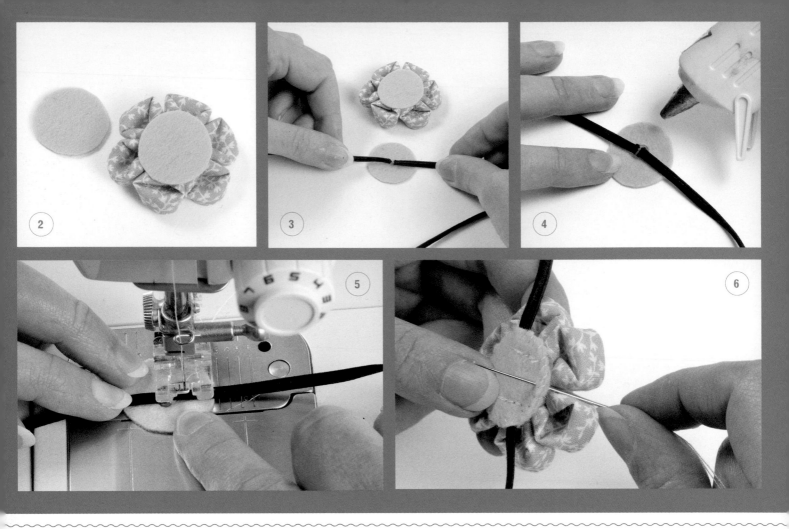

1. Wrap a measuring tape around your head, as if it were a headband. Wrap it comfortably, but only slightly snug—nothing's more uncomfortable than an overly tight headband! Take this measurement and cut a piece of elastic cord to the same length.

2. Make a flower using the Basic Instructions in Chapter 2. Cut two circles from felt that are the same size and large enough to cover the center back of your flower without being visible from the front. Glue one of the circles to the back of the flower with hot glue.

3. Place the ends of the elastic cord on the other felt circle, as shown. Make sure the rest of the cord is not twisted because you want it to lay flat against your head.

4. You're going to machine-sew the ends of the cord to the felt circle, but I find this is easier to do if you first tack the

elastic to the felt. Use a very small spot of hot glue for this, and place the ends of the elastic over it, as shown. Let the glue set for a minute. (Use the hot glue sparingly, as it can be challenging to sew over a dollop of dried glue that's too large.)

5. Set your sewing machine to a 2" stitch length. Stitch across both ends of the elastic, as shown, sewing both forward and backwards to make them extra secure.

6. Now take the flower with its felt-circle backing. Match the felt circle on the flower with the felt circle on the elastic, and stitch them together by hand using a tiny whipstitch.

Optional Step: If you want to add another flower to the headband, repeat Steps 4 and 5 and sew another felt circle to the elastic, positioning it where you want the next flower to sit. Then repeat Step 6 to attach another flower.

You can use the same technique to make a stretchy ponytail holder. In fact, you can use a ready-made elastic ponytail holder, which makes securing the elastic to the felt much easier. Or modify this design to make a comfortable, flexible flower bracelet.

Or,
Try This...

Fuzzy-Flower Scarf

You can, of course, make your Kanzashi out of fabrics other than cotton. Here, I've felted a thrift-store cashmere sweater, cut it into squares, and made these soft, appealing flowers. They make a warm embellishment for a wool scarf, or a knitted, crocheted, or felted scarf, for that matter!

Before You Begin

- Browse your local thrift stores for old sweaters that are at least 90% cashmere or angora, or a blend of these. To felt a sweater, wash it in a top-loading washing machine in hot water with a little soap. Then dry it in the dryer. Repeat this process two or three times until your sweater has shrunk and you can no longer see the knit stitches in the fabric.
- Round petals adapt most easily to sweater fabric, but you can also try a Pointed petal design.
- All seam allowances for this project are $5/8$".

Skill Level
Intermediate

Best Petal Styles
Round, modified

Best Number of Petals
5–6

Best Square Size
Sweater fabric is bulky, so stick with larger squares and fewer petals. Here I've used $2^3/_4$" and $3^1/_4$" squares.

Glues Needed
Hot glue, embellishment glue, fabric glue

Additional Supplies Needed
- 1 yard of lightweight wool, 65" wide
- Scraps of wool felt for leaves
- Coordinating thread and hand-sewing needle
- Sharp scissors
- Straight pins
- Measuring tape
- Sewing machine
- Chopstick
- Hot iron

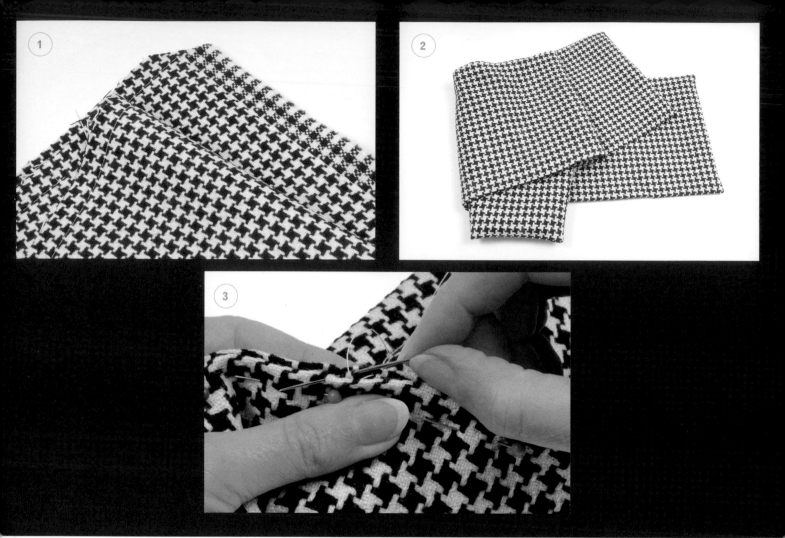

MAKING A SCARF

1. Cut a 17 × 56" rectangle from the wool. Fold it in half lengthwise, right sides together, and pin the edges together on all three sides. Sew the three sides together, leaving a 6 to 8" gap in the seam on the long side. After sewing, trim the seam allowances from all four corners, so they'll be nice and sharp when turned right-side out.

2. Use the gap in the long seam to turn the scarf right-side out, poking a chopstick into the corners to ensure that they're nice and sharp. Press the scarf flat with a hot iron.

3. Turn the raw edges of the gap to the inside and press. Sew the gap closed using tiny whipstitches.

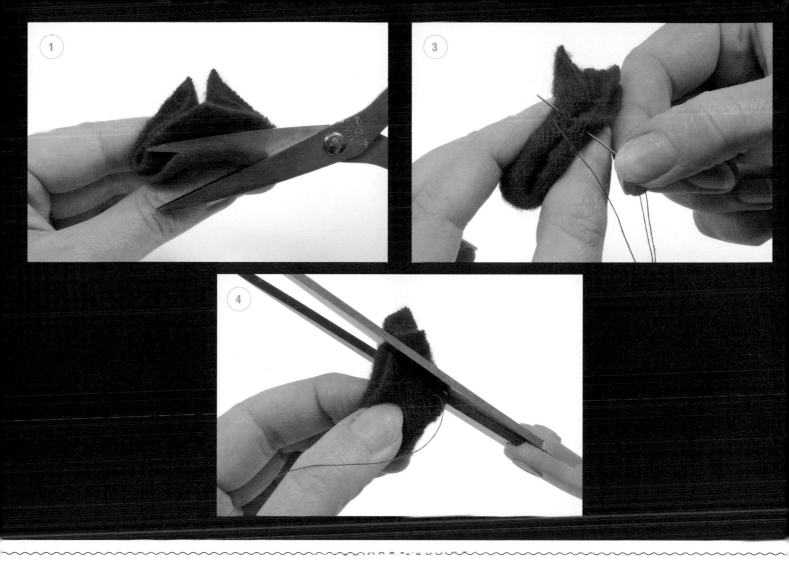

MAKING A SWEATER FLOWER

Because sweater fabric is so bulky, we need to make a few adjustments to the Basic Instructions for Round petals in Chapter 2. Begin by following Steps 1–4 of the Basic Instructions, as usual.

1. We need to remove a little bulk from each petal. Here, I'm holding the folded square from Step 4 of the Basic Instructions. On the back side of the square, cut away the bottom part of the topmost layer, as shown.

2. To continue folding the petal, proceed with Steps 5–7 of the Basic Instructions in Chapter 2. With that bulky sweater fabric, this may take a little practice. Remember to hold the fabric firmly. You can stretch it a little if you need to in order to get it into the proper shape.

3. Instead of sticking a pin through the finished petal, we're going to stitch it together. So, starting at the center of the back of the petal, sew the folds together with a whipstitch. Make sure you're sewing from the center toward the bottom of the petal. These stitches will be entirely hidden, so don't worry about being too neat.

4. Stop after you've sewn down to about $1/4$" from the bottom edge of the petal, and leave the needle and thread attached. Now trim off the bottom edge of the petal as you normally would in order to assemble a flower.

(continued)

5. Pick up your needle again and continue whipstitching. Stitch the bottom edges of the petal together. When you get to about $1/4$" from the front of the petal, stop again. Keep the needle and thread attached.

6. Notice how the center front of the petal is a little taller than the rest of the petal? This is because of the bulk of the fabric. Just tuck in this raised edge with your finger and finish stitching the bottom of the petal together. You'll then have a little pleat at the base of the petal. Repeat Steps 1–6 to make the remaining petals, and then assemble two flowers according to the Basic Flower Assembly instructions in Chapter 2.

7. Cut out some leaves from your felt scraps, and sew them to the backs of your finished flowers using a tiny whipstitch. Again, this stitching won't be visible in the finished scarf.

8. Attach the flowers to the scarf by applying a little fabric glue to the back of each flower and pressing it into place on the scarf. Allow the glue to dry. Then attach the outside edges of each petal to the scarf using a tiny whipstitch.

You can always make a sweater-flower brooch or two to embellish your favorite sweater. Wool felt is also a lovely fabric for Kanzashi—here's a scarf that's decorated with cheery wool felt flowers.

Dressed-up Denim Skirt

Who doesn't love a basic denim skirt? It goes with just about everything in your closet. Here's a way to make that wardrobe staple more unique: Add some Kanzashi flowers. We'll attach them with snaps, so you can pop them off before you pop your skirt in the wash. As an additional bit of fun, we'll learn to make some simple Kanzashi leaves, which you can use to embellish any project in this book!

Before You Begin

- This project requires a ready-made denim skirt, but you could also make your own using your favorite pattern.
- Begin this project by making three flowers in assorted sizes. You can use a shade of denim to match your skirt or a contrasting shade.
- The centers of these flowers are made with buttons covered in coordinating denim. You could use any buttons you like—just make sure they're large enough to adequately cover the centers of your flowers.

Skill Level
Intermediate

Best Petal Styles
Round, Pointed, Pleated (I'm using Pointed and Pleated here.)

Best Number of Petals
6–10

Best Square Size
I've used $3^1/_2$", 3", and $2^1/_2$"

Glues Needed
Hot glue, fabric glue

Additional Supplies Needed

- Denim skirt
- $^1/_8$ yard each of lightweight denim in 2–3 shades, for flowers and leaves
- Hand-sewing needle and coordinating thread
- Straight pins
- Fray Check
- Washable white fabric-marking pencil
- Sew-on snaps in sizes 10 and 7
- Covered button kits (I've used $1^1/_2$", $1^1/_8$", and $^3/_4$".)
- Sew-on $^1/_2$" black Velcro dots (optional)
- Sharp scissors
- Hot iron

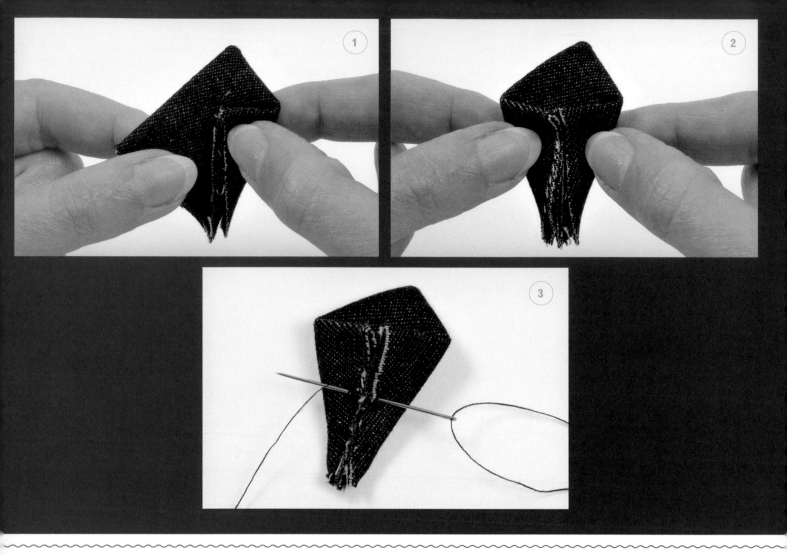

MAKING KANZASHI LEAVES

For this project, we're going to add a little foliage to our flowers. This simple leaf can be used with any Kanzashi project in this book. Play around with various sizes of squares until you find a leaf size you like for your flower.

1. Begin with the Basic Instructions for folding a Round petal in Chapter 2, proceeding through Step 4. Looking at the back side of the folded square, fold the right side toward the center, as shown. Press this fold in place with a hot iron.

2. Fold the left side of the square toward the center as well. Press this fold.

3. Sew the center back flaps of the leaf together, using small stitches through both sides, as shown. These stitches will be hidden in the finished skirt, so don't worry too much about making them perfect.

4. Place the leaf against the back of a flower, as shown, so that the front of the leaf is peeking out from the edge of the front of the flower. Attach the leaf to the back of the flower with a tiny whipstitch, making tiny stitches in both the petal and the back of the flower, as shown. Here, too, these stitches will be hidden later. Apply one or two leaves to each of the three flowers in this manner.

5. Cut three circles from the denim skirt, sized to cover the backs of the three flowers. Apply some Fray Check to the edges.

6. Sew the flat side of a snap to the center of each circle. I used these snap sizes: size 10 snap for the 3^{1}/$_{2}$" and 3" flowers, and size 7 snap for the 2^{1}/$_{2}$" flower.

7. Attach a finished circle to the center back of each flower, matching up the correct size snap to each flower. A simple method is to first apply a little fabric glue to the center back of the flower and to press the circle into it. Allow this to dry. Then sew the edges of the circle securely to the back of the flower with tiny stitches, as shown.

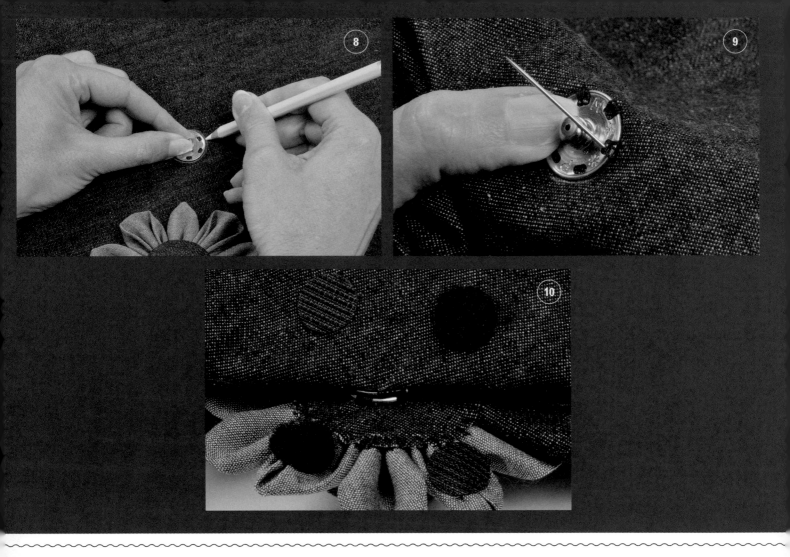

8. Lay out your skirt on a large flat surface, front side facing up. Place the flowers on the skirt, moving them around until you achieve your desired configuration. You'll need to attach a snap to the skirt where each flower will be. Use a fabric-marking pencil to trace around each snap.

9. Sew the snaps securely to the front of the skirt. The traced circle will help keep them from sliding out of position while you're sewing.

10. Snap the flowers to the skirt. Hang the skirt from a skirt hanger, or simply hold it up to yourself, and take a look at how the flowers hang. Larger flowers are a bit heavy and will tend to droop forward when you wear the skirt. If you see this happening, just stitch a Velcro dot or two to the top of the flower and to the skirt. These dots will invisibly help the flower lay flat.

Adorn a tweed or corduroy jacket with a matching Kanzashi brooch — very smart-looking! If you sew your own jacket, you can make a flower from the leftover fabric. If you buy a ready-made jacket, you can look for some fabric that matches. And wouldn't it be fun to use this technique to trim a blouse with some matching Kanzashi?

Or,
Try This...

Happiest Belt Buckle Ever

If you're feeling adventurous, try making this adorable belt buckle. The flower is made from upholstery vinyl, which takes a little practice to work with but has lots of fun applications. You can usually find upholstery vinyl at fabric stores that sell home decor fabrics, or you can ask your local upholstery shop for scraps.

Before You Begin

- Be sure to protect your work surface, and be careful not to use too much glue. If either superglue or E6000 oozes out of your work, you can easily end up permanently sticking a binder clip to your flower or—worse—gluing your flower to the work surface!
- It's good to note that superglue cannot do the same job as E6000. Superglue makes a brittle bond when it dries, so don't use it for any of the steps that specifically call for E6000.
- You can usually find webbing belts and metal buckles at fabric stores or army surplus stores.

Skill Level
Advanced

Best Petal Styles
Round, with some modifications

Best Number of Petals
8

Best Square Size
$2^3/_4$"

Glue Needed
Superglue, E6000

Additional Supplies Needed
- $^1/_8$ yard (or scraps) upholstery vinyl
- $1^1/_2$"-diameter shank button
- Approximately 1 yard $1^1/_4$" cotton belt webbing
- One $1^3/_8$" metal web belt buckle
- Very strong scissors (you'll be cutting through several layers of vinyl at once)
- Eight large binder clips
- Paper or cardboard for work surface

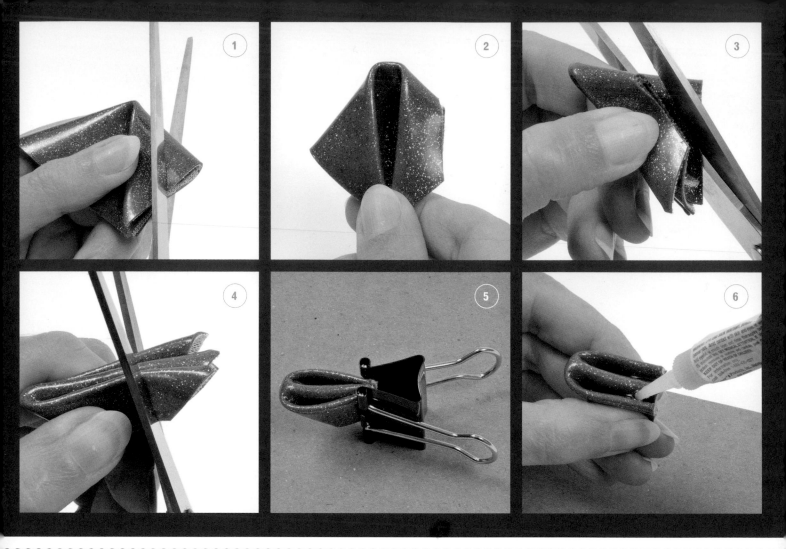

MAKING A VINYL PETAL

1. First we're going to modify the Round petal fold. Follow the Basic Instructions in Chapter 2 through Step 3. Then carefully trim off about $1/2$" of the right-hand corner, as shown.

2. Fold the left-hand corner of the petal down, as in Step 4 of the Basic Instructions.

3. Fold the petal in half, as shown. Using the edge you cut in Step 1 as a guide, cut away the remaining corner.

4. Cut off the bottom $1/2$" of the petal. (Note: This is a little more than you normally trim off when making a fabric petal.)

5. Place a binder clip on the end of the petal to hold it. Over the next several steps, you'll briefly remove this binder clip, apply glue, and then replace it. Place some paper or cardboard over your work surface.

6. We'll use superglue to hold the petal together, and we'll glue it in stages, because the vinyl is stiff and wants to unfold itself. Begin by removing the binder clip and holding the petal firmly so it doesn't unfold. Place a drop of superglue between the folds on the front of the petal, as shown. Immediately replace the binder clip on the end of the petal, and let that sit for about two minutes, allowing the superglue to fully bond.

ASSEMBLING A VINYL FLOWER

7. Remove the binder clip again and turn the petal over to the back. (No need to hold the petal together at this point.) Place a drop of superglue in the center fold of the back, as shown. Replace the binder clip for a minute so that the superglue can fully bond.

8. Remove the binder clip once again. You should now see the remaining loose edges of your petal opening up, as shown. Place a drop of superglue in each opening, and then replace the binder clip. Give the superglue a minute to bond. Repeat Steps 1–8 to make seven more petals.

1. Cut a $2^1/_2$"-diameter circle of vinyl to form the base of your flower. (This is a larger circle than we usually cut for the back of a fabric flower; since we're using vinyl, we need a larger base in order to glue the bottoms of the petals to it.) Assemble your petals around the circle, as shown. The bottom edges of the petals should be touching. Look at the outer tips of the petals: Are there large gaps between them, like you see here? Then you may need to trim a little more from the bases of your petals so that you can nestle them closer together.

2. Remove the petals from the vinyl circle and set them aside for a moment. Apply a thick ring of E6000 glue to the circle, keeping it about $^1/_2$" away from the edge.

(continued)

3. Carefully place the petals in the glue, adjusting them until they are evenly spaced around the circle. (E6000 takes a long time to set, so you'll have plenty of time to adjust the petals to your liking.)

4. Once you have the petals arranged the way you like them, you'll need a weight to hold them in place while the glue sets. The weight should be about an inch larger in diameter than the center opening of the flower. I like to use a large shot glass filled with loose change. You can also use the cap from a spray can. Place the weight on the flower, and then check on it often for the first ten minutes to make sure nothing slides out of place. If you find that the petals are sliding, then the weight is too heavy. Lighten it a bit, and then watch it for another ten minutes. Then leave the flower alone for twenty-four hours, until the E6000 has set completely.

5. The next day, use E6000 to glue a large, flat button over the center hole of your flower. Place a weight on top of the flower as you did in Step 4, and leave it for one to two hours while the glue sets.

ASSEMBLING A BELT BUCKLE

1. Remove the buckle from the belt. Use E6000 to glue your finished flower to the center front of the buckle. Allow the glue to dry completely.

2. Wrap the belt around your waist. The ends of the belt should overlap by about 6". Cut away any excess. Web belts usually come with a metal tip to cover the end of the belt, so when you have your desired belt length, wrap this tip over one end and close it.

3. Slide the buckle onto the other end of the belt and move the slider to lock it in place.

If you can make a flower from vinyl, you can make one from leather — or pleather (plastic leather)! Imagine how cool this leather flower would look pinned to a cowboy hat, a wool coat, or a purse.

Or,
Try This...

Super Star Tote

You can make more than just flowers with the basic petal folds in this book—such as this five-pointed star. It makes a cute, beachy motif for a pretty tote bag.

Before You Begin

- If you like, you can always start with a ready-made tote bag and just embellish it with these stars.
- Be careful with fabric-marking pens and pencils—usually, the heat from the iron will set the marks so they can't be removed later. Follow the package instructions for your marker carefully.
- All seam allowances for this project are $1/4$" unless otherwise specified.

Skill Level
Intermediate

Best Petal Styles
Pointed, modified

Best Number of Petals
5

Best Square Size
Any (I'm using $3^{1}/_{2}$" here.)

Glues Needed
Hot glue, fabric glue

Additional Supplies Needed
- $3/_4$ yard medium-weight cotton canvas
- $1/_2$ yard coordinating heavyweight cotton print
- Washable fabric-marking pen
- Hand-sewing needle and coordinating thread
- Straight pins
- Sharp scissors
- Sewing machine
- Ruler or measuring tape
- Hot iron

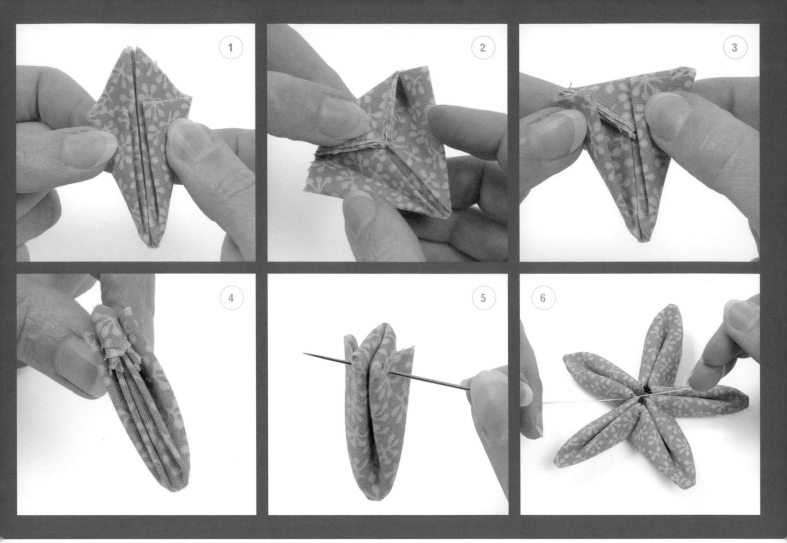

MAKING KANZASHI STARS

1. Use the Basic Instructions in Chapter 2 to make five Pointed petals, but don't trim off the ends as usual. Instead, we're going to modify them a little. At the back of the petal, open it flat, as shown.

2. Now briefly unfold the two sides, and then fold the tip over, as shown.

3. Refold these sides over the fold you made in Step 2, as shown.

4. Fold the petal in half again. (We're looking at the back of the petal here.) The purpose of this little modification is to add some extra bulk at the base of the petal, which helps it maintain the star shape.

5. Assemble the five petals according to the instructions in Basic Flower Assembly in Chapter 2, but with this modification: When you string each petal, insert the needle through it closer to the front of the petal than the back, as shown. This helps give the star more width at its center.

6. When you tie the star together, leave a small opening in the center, as shown. Hot-glue a circle of the same fabric you used for the stars to the back as well. Make sure this circle is small enough so that it doesn't show from the front.

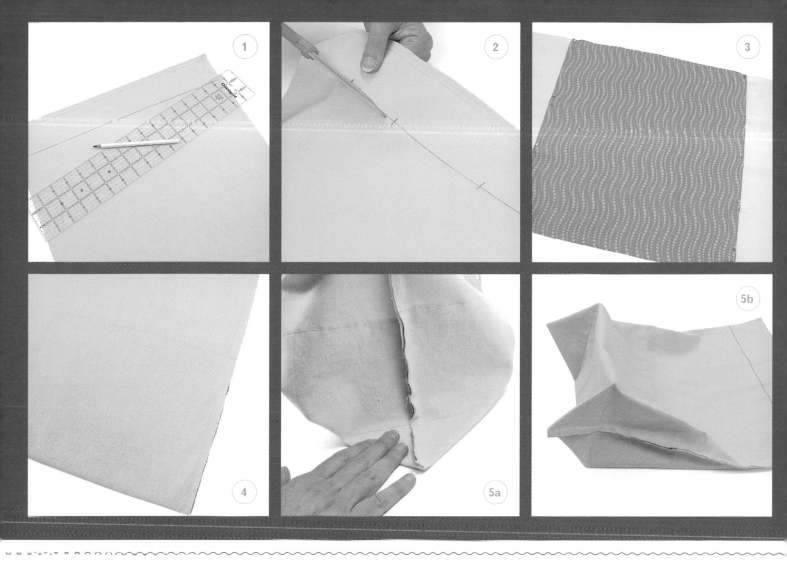

MAKING A TOTE

1. Cut a rectangle from the cotton canvas that measures 16 × 36". Using a fabric-marking pen, mark a line on the wrong side of the fabric 3" from one of the 16" edges. Next turn under ¼" of fabric along this edge and stitch. Do the same thing with the other 16" edge.

2. Mark these 16" edges again: 3½" in from each edge, and then 2½" from each side of the center. Cut a 2" slit in the fabric between each set of marks. Repeat this step on the other 16" edge. You should end up with four slits altogether—two at each end of the rectangle.

3. Cut a square from the coordinating cotton fabric that measures 16 × 16". Turn under ¼" of fabric along two opposite edges, and press. Position this cotton panel on top of the

canvas panel, matching raw edges and centering the cotton panel along the 36" length of the canvas. Pin the two pieces together, with the right sides of both facing up. Machine-sew them together by stitching close to the folded edges of the cotton panel.

4. Fold the tote in half, right sides together, matching the two 16" edges. (The 16" edges are actually the top edge of your tote and will not be sewn in this step.) Pin the side edges together and press a crease into the bottom of the bag. Sew up both side seams.

5a and 5b. Now make a square bottom for the bag. Flatten out the corner of one side seam, as shown in **a**. Make sure the seam lines up with the crease you pressed into the bottom of

(continued)

85

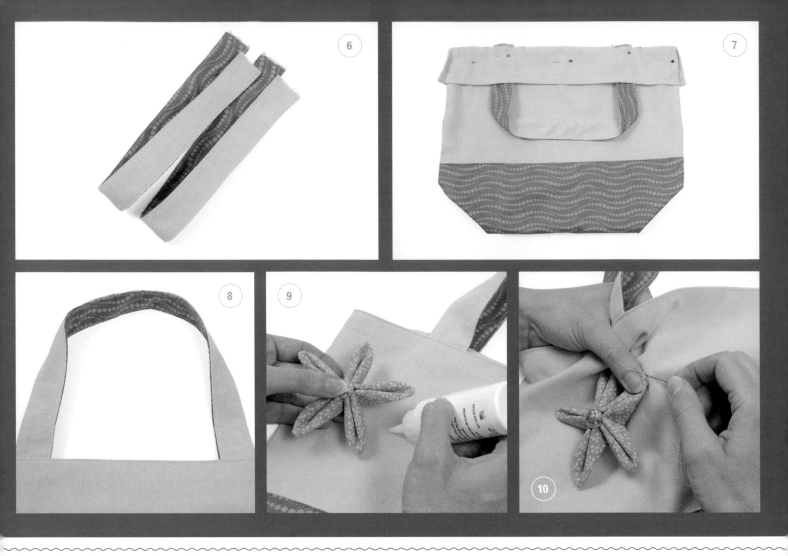

the bag in Step 4. Use a ruler to find the spot where there is 2¹/₂" of fabric on each side of the seam, as shown. Draw a line with the fabric marker across the corner of the bag at this location. Machine-sew along this line, as shown in **b**. Repeat this step with the other corner of the bag.

6. To make straps for your bag, cut two pieces of canvas and two pieces of cotton, each measuring 3¹/₂ × 19". Pair up one cotton and one canvas piece, right sides together. Machine-sew them together along both 19" edges. Turn them right-side out and press them flat. Topstitch close to all 19" edges. Repeat with the remaining pieces.

7. Turn the bag right-side out. Fold the top of the bag down to the outside along the lines you drew in Step 1. Insert the ends of your handles into the four slits you cut in Step 2, as

shown. Pin them in place. Sew along the folded edge at the top of the bag, using a ⁵/₈" seam allowance. You'll catch the ends of the handles in this seam, attaching them to the bag.

8. Turn this seam toward the inside, which will also bring the handles to the top of the bag. Press along the folded edge, and then topstitch close to this edge.

9. Decide where you want to place the Kanzashi stars on your finished bag. Tack them in place by putting a small amount of fabric glue on the center back of each star and gently pressing it onto the bag. Allow them to dry completely.

10. Using a tiny whipstitch, hand-sew each of the five points of each star to the bag.

That star shape, made small and adorned with some little comet-tails of ribbon, can be fashioned into a very cute Shooting Star Brooch. Not to mention the fact that you can adorn most of the projects in this book with Kanzashi stars instead of flowers!

*Or,
Try This...*

Handbag Candy

Kanzashi look so cute dangling from your handbag or tote! This flower-charm is designed to be easy to move from bag to bag as the mood strikes you. It also makes use of a fantastic design technique you'll be learning here: layering two Kanzashi together to make one elaborate flower.

Before You Begin

- Depending on the size and shape of your handbag, you may opt to shorten or lengthen the chain a little.

Skill Level
Intermediate

Best Petal Styles
Round, Pleated, Pointed

Best Number of Petals
8–10

Best Square Size
You can use any size you like, depending on the design of your flower. I've used $3^1/_4$" and $1^1/_2$" squares here.

Glues Needed
Hot glue, embellishment glue, fabric glue

Additional Supplies Needed
- Scrap of wool felt
- Two 24-gauge eye pins, at least 1" long
- Three 8-mm jump rings
- Small lobster clasp
- 3" medium-width link chain
- Sharp scissors
- Wire cutters
- Needle-nose pliers

MAKING A LAYERED FLOWER

1. Fold and assemble two flowers, using the Basic Instructions in Chapter 2. One should be at least 1" smaller in diameter than the other. Don't put any centers on them just yet.

2. Take the larger flower and gently adjust its shape so that its top surface is flat. If your larger flower is made with Round petals, then you won't need to do this step; but Pointed or Pleated petals are taller at the center than at the ends, so they tend to be domed in the middle and require a little adjustment. Once you've completed this step, the back of your larger flower will be slightly dome-shaped.

3. Now that you have a flat front surface on the larger flower, you can glue the smaller flower on top of it. Apply fabric glue to the center of the larger flower and gently press the smaller flower on top. Allow the glue to dry. Then use embellishment glue to add a center to your flower.

MAKING A BAUBLE

1. Using needle-nose pliers, carefully open a jump ring. String one of the eye pins onto it and close the jump ring. Do the same with the other eye pin and jump ring.

2. Cut a 2"-diameter circle from wool felt. Apply a thick ring of embellishment glue to the felt, keeping the glue about $1/4$" from the edges. Position the two eye pins on the felt, as shown. The eyes should stick out just beyond the edge

of the felt, and the bottoms of the pins should meet but not cross. You may need to trim your eye pins a little before you glue them to get them into this configuration.

3. Press the felt to the back of the flower. Make sure that the eye pins and jump rings are positioned so that they are on either side of the topmost petal of your flower. Allow the glue to dry completely before proceeding.

(continued)

4. Cut a 3" length of chain. Using needle-nose pliers, open a new jump ring. Thread the ring through the end link of the chain and then through the lobster clasp. Close the jump ring.

5. Reopen the left-hand jump ring that's attached to the back of the flower, thread it through the other end link of the chain, and reclose it.

6. To attach this bauble to a handbag, simply wrap the chain around one handle or strap and fasten the lobster clasp to the jump ring.

Layered Kanzashi make absolutely stunning brooches. Or adornments for
pendants, or tote bags, or . . . well, pretty much any project in this book!

Or,
Try This...

4

Projects to Give

Once you become comfortable making Kanzashi flowers, you'll want to surround yourself with them. These projects will help you do just that—and perhaps help you surround the people on your gift list, too. It's so easy to create a pretty Kanzashi Bouquet (page 100) to brighten your nightstand, or some Back-to-Back Ornaments (page 96) to hang in a sunny window. If you're feeling more adventurous, try using your Kanzashi skills in a whole new way by making some Butterfly Jar Toppers (page 116)—a lovely way to store your buttons, beads, and ribbons!

Back-to-Back Ornament

These generous-sized Kanzashi flowers make lovely decorations for your holiday tree, or you can use them to brighten a window. These are so showy that you can use your biggest, most elaborate buttons as centers. And because you are attaching two flowers back-to-back, you can display these from either side.

Before You Begin

- As you string the petals of your flowers for this project, pay special attention. When you place your flowers back-to-back, you'll want all the petals to match up neatly, so be very consistent about where you pass your needle through each petal.

Skill Level
Beginner

Best Petal Styles
Round, Pointed, Pleated

Best Number of Petals
8 or more

Best Square Size
2¹/₂" to 3"

Glues Needed
Hot glue, embellishment glue, fabric glue

Additional Supplies Needed
- Straight pins (optional)
- Pearl embroidery floss in a color that coordinates with your flower (DMC Metallic Gold floss used here)
- Sharp scissors

MAKING AN ORNAMENT

1. Make two flowers, following the Basic Instructions in Chapter 2. You can certainly make them in different colors, and with different centers, but you'll want them to have the same petal design and size so that you can match them up. Glue a center to each flower with embellishment glue.

2. Cut an 8" length of floss. Fold it in half and tie a knot about 1" from the end. Place one flower face down on your work surface. Apply some fabric glue to the back of the flower and lay the knotted floss over the glue, as shown. Be sure that the looped end of the floss lines up with the topmost petal, as shown.

3. Place the second flower atop the first so that their back sides are glued together, with the floss sandwiched in the middle. Make sure all the petals of both flowers are aligned. Allow the glue to dry completely.

4. Depending on your flower design, you might want to glue the two flowers together at the tips of the petals. If you do, then carefully apply a small amount of fabric glue between each set of petals and gently press them together.

5. If the petals have a tendency to split apart while drying, you can stick a straight pin through them to hold them in place. Just stick them through the middle of each pair of petals, away from the glue, as shown. Allow the glue to dry completely.

You can use the same technique to make a charming flower garland. Just sandwich some ribbon between a string of smaller flowers. Or, for a lighter garland, you can sandwich the ribbon between one flower and one circle of coordinating felt. This would look so cute draped over a simple window shade!

Or,
Try This...

Kanzashi Bouquet

It's easy to add stems to your flowers, after which you can fill a vase with them! Make your flowers from bright cottons, and they're perfect for a little girl's room. Or make them from an elegant, slubby silk blend like these to add a sophisticated accent to your home decor.

~~~~~~~~~~~~~~~~~~~~~~~~~~~~~~~~

Before You Begin
- Floral stem wire comes precut in 18" pieces rather than wrapped around a paddle. You can find it and the green floral tape at craft stores, or check the Resources section for online suppliers.
- Hot glue is a good choice for attaching flowers to wire stems because it sets so quickly.

Skill Level
Beginner

Best Petal Styles
Round, Pointed, Pleated

Best Number of Petals
6–10

Best Square Size
2–3$^1/_2$"

Glues Needed
Hot glue, embellishment glue

Additional Supplies Needed
- 20-gauge floral stem wire
- Green floral tape
- Faux pearl-head stamens (optional)
- Sharp scissors

ADDING A STAMEN CENTER

a. Using double-ended stamens, fold them in half and insert them into the folds of the petals. (Fold them a little unevenly, so the stamens will be different lengths in the finished flower.) Keep them very close to the center of the flower. Glue a center onto your flower with embellishment glue, which will ooze into the petals and seal in the stamens.

MAKING A STEMMED FLOWER

1. Make a flower, using the Basic Instructions in Chapter 2. Cut two circles of the same fabric for the back of your flower. Glue one to the flower. Cut a slit into the other, from one edge to the center, as shown.

2. Take a strand of floral stem wire and bend one end into a 2" loop. Twist the wire to secure this loop. Then wrap the wire below the loop with floral tape.

3. Bend the looped end of the wire at a 90-degree angle. Shape the loop into a circle with your fingers, as shown.

4. Apply some hot glue to the back of the flower and place the wire into the glue.

5. Quickly press the second fabric circle over the wire. The slit you cut into this circle in Step 1 will allow you to place it so the wire is in the center, as shown.

Or, Try This...

By slightly modifying these instructions, you can also make tall, spiky flowers. Just put two wrapped pieces of wire together and twist them so that you leave an open loop every couple of inches. Then glue small flowers back-to-back at those loops (see the photo on page 20 for a closer look at this process). *Voilà!*

Sampler Wall Hanging

This project started with the buttons. I found a small collection of carved shell buttons at a thrift store; they were all different, but looked lovely together. So I thought, "Why not do the same thing with flowers?" I love the way this wall hanging presents a group of Kanzashi as if it were a collection of butterflies—in a nice, orderly grid. You could also display this design in a shadowbox frame.

Before You Begin

- For the flowers that adorn this wall hanging, I chose nine fabrics that coordinate well. That gave me plenty of variety, and the flowers still complement one another visually.
- Be careful with fabric-marking pens and pencils: Usually, the heat from your iron will set the marks so they can't be removed later. Follow the package instructions for your marker.
- All the machine sewing in this project uses a $^1/_4$" seam allowance unless otherwise specified.

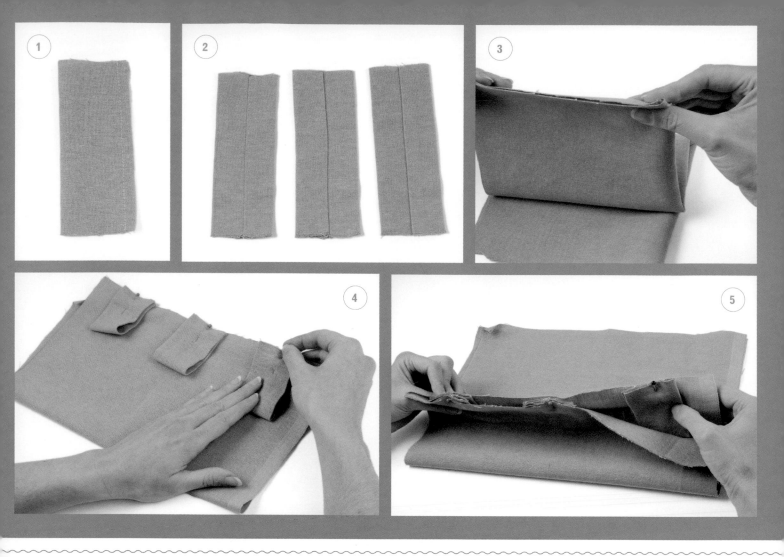

MAKING A WALL HANGING

1. Cut the following pieces from your canvas: two rectangles measuring 14 × 15", and three rectangles measuring 5 × 6". Fold the three 5 × 6" pieces in half, right sides together, so that the 6" edges meet. Sew along these edges. When you're done, you should have three fabric tubes.

2. Turn these tubes right-side out and press each one flat so that the seams are in the center, as shown. These tubes are the three tabs that will appear along the top of your wall hanging. They will be folded so that the seams stay on the inside, unseen.

3. Take one of the 14 × 15" pieces of fabric. Fold it in half along the 14" edge to find the center, and place a pin there. Flatten it back out.

4. Take one of the tabs you made in Step 2 and fold it in half, with the seam to the inside. Pin the folded tab to the center of the fabric panel, matching raw edges. Measure 1³/₄" in from the left-hand corner of the panel. Place the second tab at this location, matching raw edges, and pin together. Repeat this process at the right-hand corner with the third tab.

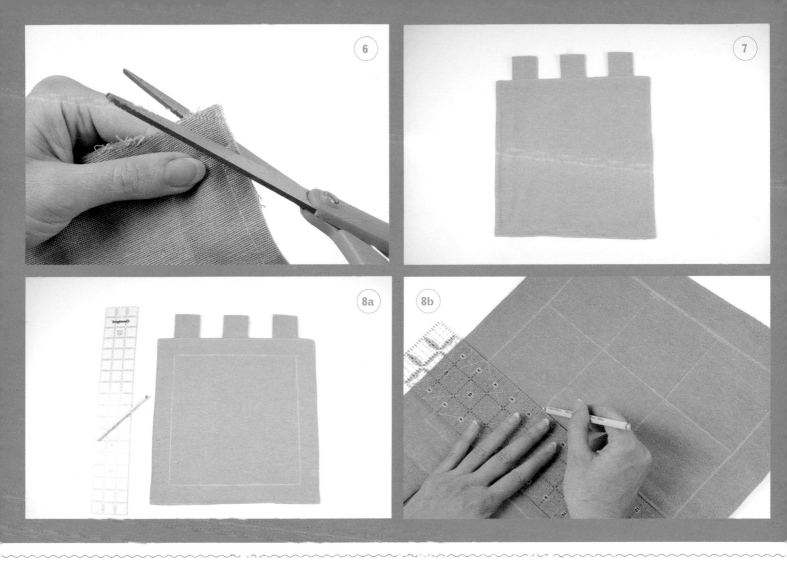

5. Place the two 14 × 15" pieces of fabric together, so that the right sides are together and the tabs are sandwiched between the two pieces. Pin the pieces together. Machine-sew along this top edge with a ⁶/₈" seam allowance, sewing across all three tabs as you do.

6. Pin the fabric together along the other three sides. Machine-sew along each side, using a ¹/₄" seam allowance and leaving a 6" gap in the bottom seam. After sewing, trim the corners, as shown.

7. Use that gap in the bottom seam to turn the whole piece right-side out. Poke the corners out from the inside with a chopstick to make them nice and sharp. Carefully flatten all the edges and press the wall hanging with a hot iron. Topstitch ¹/₈" from all four edges.

8a and 8b. Use your fabric-marking pencil and a ruler to draw a nine-square grid on the front of your wall hanging. The outer edges of the grid should be 1¹/₂" from the edges of the wall hanging. Each square should be approximately 3¹/₂".

(continued)

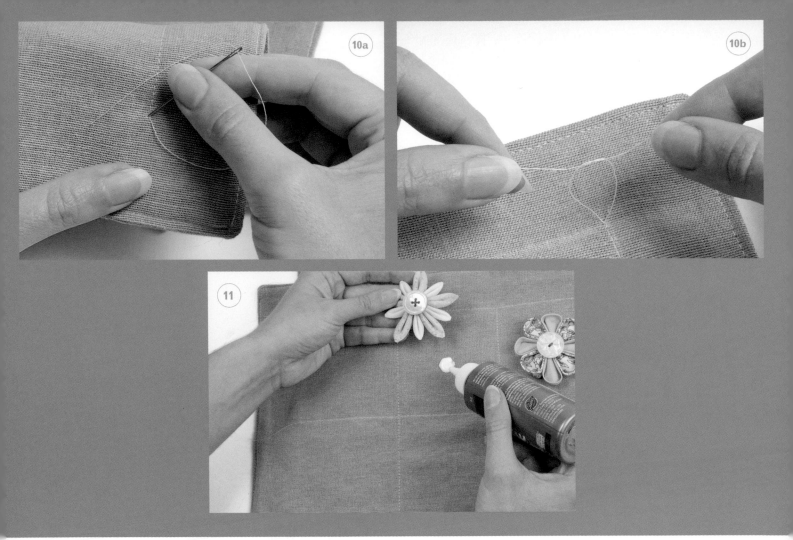

9. Use contrasting thread to topstitch the grid through both layers of fabric, sewing along your drawn lines. To make these lines neat and precise, don't use your sewing machine's backstitch function to start and end your seams. Instead, try the tip in Step 10.

10a and 10b. Leave long threads at the start and finish of each row of topstitching **(a)**. When you're done machine-sewing the grid lines, you can thread the strands that are on the front of the fabric onto a hand-sewing needle and pull them through to the back. On the back of the fabric,

tie the two strands into a double knot and trim off the end **(b)**. Remove the pencil marks from the front of the wall hanging, following the package directions for your fabric-marking pencil.

11. Make nine Kanzashi flowers, following the Basic Instructions in Chapter 2. You can follow the petal combinations in the photograph, or come up with your own. Glue a center to each flower with embellishment glue. Use fabric glue to adhere one flower to the center of each square in the grid pattern. Allow the glue to dry thoroughly before hanging.

This "sampler" design is also cute as a tote bag. You can follow the instructions for the Super Star Tote on page 82. Before you sew up the side seams of your tote, mark and stitch your grid onto the front panel. You can make your grid with large squares or smaller, too.

Or, Try This...

Elegant Floral Gift Topper

Dress up even the simplest gift with this dazzling tie-on Kanzashi. The dangling elements you see here are often seen on traditional Japanese Kanzashi, where they're called "falls." You can make the falls as long or short as you like. And if you want to be really clever, you can add a pin-back to the fabric flower before you tie it to the gift. That way, the recipient can simply snip off the ribbon and wear your creation.

Before You Begin
- If you're making very small falls, then you might want to use some of the techniques for working with miniature flowers from the Tiny Blossom Earrings project on page 44.

page 44

Skill Level
Intermediate

Best Petal Styles
Round, Pointed, or Pleated

Best Number of Petals
6–10

Best Square Size
I've used $3\frac{1}{2}$" squares to make the flower and $1\frac{1}{2}$" squares to make the falls. You could make this design larger or smaller according to the size of the package you're topping.

Glues Needed
Hot glue, fabric glue, embellishment glue

Additional Supplies Needed
- $\frac{1}{2}$ yard each of two coordinating colors of $\frac{1}{4}$" satin ribbon, plus enough extra of one color to tie around your package
- Scrap of coordinating wool felt
- Self-fabric for backing
- 1" pin-back (optional)
- Straight pins
- Sharp scissors
- Hot iron

MAKING A FALL

1. Have a hot iron handy while you fold the petals for your falls. Begin by folding a 1½" square in half diagonally, with the right side of the fabric facing out. Press this fold.

2. Open the square flat again. Fold it in half diagonally in the opposite direction. Press that fold, and then open the square flat again. Your square should now have an X-shaped crease across the center.

3. Now fold each of the four corners of the square in toward the center, pressing each fold in place.

4. Fold the resulting square in half diagonally so that all the raw edges are folded toward the inside. Press this fold in place.

5. Fold this triangle in half crosswise. Press this fold in place.

6. Hold your petal in place with a pin. Repeat Steps 1–6 to make as many petals for your fall as you like. Cut a length of ribbon 4" longer than you want your finished fall to be.

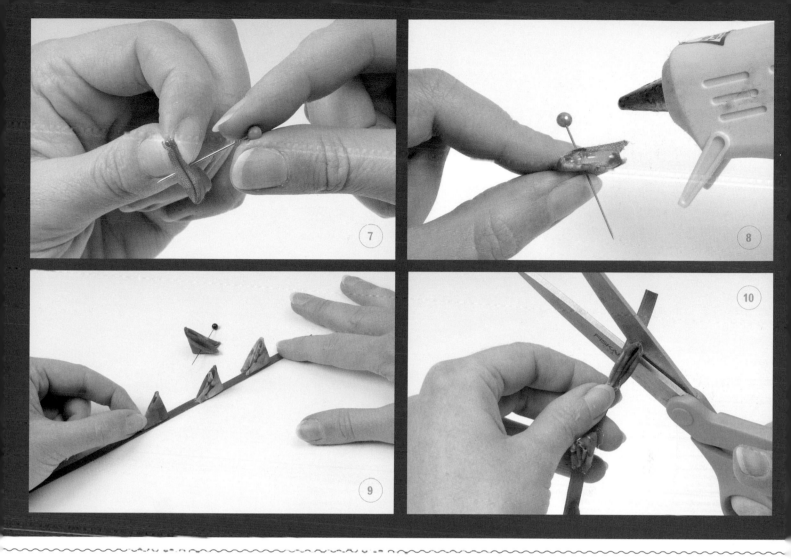

7. Take a petal and pinch the tip in your fingers, as shown. Since fall petals are small, you may choose to leave in the pin as you proceed to the next step, or you may choose to remove it. Try both ways and see which feels more comfortable to you.

8. Apply a thin line of hot glue to the edge of the petal, making sure some glue gets on both sides of the edge.

9. Quickly remove the pin (if you've left it in) and gently press this edge onto the ribbon. The first petal of your fall should be located at least 3" below the top of the ribbon to accommodate the flower. Repeat Steps 8 and 9 as many times as needed to add all the petals to your fall. You can space them close together along the ribbon, or farther apart. You can also glue petals to one side of the ribbon or both. Make sure that they all face the same direction!

10. Trim the end of the ribbon close to the bottom petal on the fall. Repeat Steps 1–10 to make as many falls as you like for your gift topper.

ASSEMBLING THE GIFT TOPPER

1. Follow the Basic Instructions in Chapter 2 to make a Kanzashi flower. Glue a circle of self-fabric (the flower fabric) to the back. Use fabric glue to attach each strand of your fall to the back of the flower. Spread them out a bit, as shown, so they'll hang separately.

2. Next take the strand of ribbon that will be wrapped around your package. Find the center by folding it in half. Then use fabric glue to adhere the center of the ribbon to the back of the flower, placing it directly over the fall ribbons.

3. Cut a circle of wool felt that has the same diameter as the self-fabric circle on the back of the flower. Apply fabric glue around all edges of the felt, and press it gently to the center back of your flower, covering all the ribbons.

If you want to make your flower into a pin, use embellishment glue to attach a pin-back to the felt circle. You can cut a smaller square from the same felt and glue that over the pin-back, as shown, for a tidier finish.

You can add falls to lots of the other flower projects in this book. Look how cute the Flower Power Pendant on page 40 looks with a little dangle! And of course you can always make beautiful gift toppers without falls.

Or, Try This...

Butterfly Jar Toppers

Here's another fun shape you can make with these Kanzashi techniques: butterflies! They make such cute toppers for these Mason jars, which is one of my favorite ways to store crafty bits and pieces such as buttons and thread.

Before You Begin

- You'll notice that this project uses a lot of different glues. I recommend using the specific glue mentioned for each step—this will result in very sturdy jar lids.
- You can often find Mason-style jars at your grocery store, in the baking section. Or, you can find vintage ones through eBay.com.
- These jars shouldn't be used to store any food or other perishable items, but they're great for dry goods.

Skill Level
Intermediate

Best Petal Styles
Round, Pointed, or Pleated

Best Number of Petals
Each butterfly wing will need 2–4 petals

Best Square Size
Any (1$^1/_2$" and 2" squares used here)

Glues Needed
Hot glue, fabric glue, E6000, embellishment glue

Additional Supplies Needed
- 24-gauge craft wire
- 4–5 beads in sizes ranging from 8-mm to 6/o seed beads (Note: They should have holes large enough to accommodate four strands of wire.)
- Hand-sewing needle and thread
- Small scrap of cardstock
- Mason-style jar with a two-part lid
- Background fabric to cover the jar lid
- Wool felt to cover the inside of the jar lid
- Sharp scissors
- Wire cutters
- Needle-nose or chain-nose pliers

MAKING A BUTTERFLY BODY

1. Cut two 12" pieces of 24-gauge craft wire. Bend these in half together at the center and give the fold a couple of twists with your fingers to create a loop, as shown.

2. Gather the four ends of the wire together, and trim them so they're the same length. Carefully thread the beads for your butterfly body through all four strands at once. Thread them in the order they'll appear in the body, with the bottom bead first. I like to use several smaller beads, followed by a few larger ones. Thread these beads all the way down the wire until they rest against the twisted loop you created in Step 1. Split the remaining lengths of wire so that you have two strands of two wires each emerging from the top of your beaded body. These will be antennae.

3. Gently twist each antenna with your fingers so that the two strands become one. Then cut each antenna to about $7/8$". Use pliers to bend the ends of each antenna into a tiny loop, as shown. Set aside your finished butterfly body while you make the wings.

ASSEMBLING A BUTTERFLY

1. Fold a series of petals in the style of your choice. I made one of these butterflies using four Round petals, and one using eight Pointed petals. You can mix and match the colors and sizes—there are endless possibilities for making butterflies! (Note: If you're using Pointed petals, trim them as you normally would for making a flower, according to the Basic Instructions in Chapter 2. If you're using Round petals, you'll need to trim them about $1/4$" shorter than you normally would for making a flower.)

2. Thread a needle with doubled thread, and tie a knot in the end. Lay the petals of each butterfly wing out in front of you, so you can easily see in what order to string them. I'm starting with the top part of the right-hand wing here. Stitch through the base of each petal (see Basic Flower Assembly instructions in Chapter 2), and slide them down the thread until they rest against the knot.

3. Stitch through both petals again to sew them together at the end. Pull the thread snug and tie a secure knot.

4a and 4b. Repeat Steps 2 and 3 to join the rest of the petals together in groups of two. If you're working with Pointed petals, you should end up with four groups of two (4a). If you're working with Round petals, you'll have two groups of two (4b). Next cut a 1" square of cardstock. This will be the base of your butterfly, but it won't be visible in

the finished project. Place this square on a protected work surface and have your hot glue gun ready.

5. Apply a wide strip of hot glue to one half of the cardstock. Gently press the two groups of petals that make up one wing into the glue, quickly adjusting them so they are positioned together snugly. Repeat the process with the other wing, and glue it to the cardstock. The two wings should be placed in a way that allows them to touch in the center.

6. Use scissors to carefully trim away any excess cardstock sticking out from the edges of the butterfly.

7. Place a spot of embellishment glue in the center of the butterfly. Carefully position the butterfly body over the glue and gently press it into place. Allow it to dry completely.

ASSEMBLING THE JAR TOPPER

1. Take the lid of your jar apart. Set the ring portion aside. Use the flat top to measure your background fabric. Cut a circle of background fabric that measures 2" larger than the diameter of the jar top.

2. Run a gathering stitch ¼" from the edge of this circle. You can hand-stitch this or sew it on a sewing machine. Be sure to leave about a 6" tail of thread so that you can pull the gathers tight in the next step.

3. Place the fabric circle wrong-side up. Place the jar lid in the center of the circle, with the rubber seal facing up. Pull on your gathering stitches to bunch the edges of the circle around the jar lid. Adjust the gathers so that they're spread evenly. When you've pleated the circle snugly around the jar lid, tie a knot in the leading ends of the gathering thread to fix the gathers in place.

4. Cut a circle of wool felt that's ¼" smaller than the diameter of the jar lid. Glue this onto the bottom of the jar lid with fabric glue, covering the gathered edges of fabric. Allow the glue to dry.

5a and 5b. I recommend gluing the two parts of your jar lid together to make it easier to use. Simply apply a little E6000 around the inside top of the ring part of the lid and then carefully place the flat part inside. Allow the glue to dry a full twenty-four hours before you twist the lid onto your jar.

6. Glue the assembled butterfly to the top of the jar lid with fabric glue. (Note: I'm showing the jar lid here before it's assembled. You can glue on the butterfly before or after you assemble the lid; just make sure you can still fit the ring section over the flat section after the butterfly is in place.)

Or, Try This...

You can apply this butterfly design to most of the flower projects in this book. Look how cute a butterfly embellishment would be on the Dressed-up Denim Skirt on page 70! And don't forget to try out some butterfly designs with the Pleated petal, too.

Recycled Necktie Wallet

Thrift-store neckties are just about my favorite craft supply. Their elegant, silky fabric and padded insides lend themselves beautifully to this simple wallet project. The Kanzashi flower is made by removing the silk cover from the tie and then cutting it into squares for folding.

Before You Begin

- Check your local thrift stores for neckties. Prices can vary wildly, but you should be able to find them for a couple of dollars each. Try eBay, too.
- I love the look of the Round petal here, but admittedly, this style might not stand up to the rigors of the inside of your purse. If you want a sturdier flower, try the Pointed petal instead.
- Most of this project is hand-sewn. I prefer hand-sewing with neckties because this method allows you to join pieces together without creating extra bulk in the seams. Just keep your stitches very small and close together, and knot your threads securely.
- If you find the necktie silk difficult to fold into petals, try fusing some lightweight interfacing to the back. Fusible interfacing is a light mesh-style fabric with a heat-activated glue on one side. When you iron it to the wrong side of another fabric, it adds a little stiffness, making the fabric easier to fold.

Skill Level
Intermediate

Best Petal Styles
Round, Pointed, Pleated

Best Number of Petals
10 or more (Since necktie silk is so thin, you'll need lots of petals to fill out your flower's shape.)

Best Square Size
$2^1/_2$" to 3"

Glue Needed
Fabric glue

Additional Supplies Needed
- Three neckties in coordinating colors, all of the same width, and at least $3^1/_2$" wide at their widest point
- Lightweight fusible interfacing (optional)
- Coordinating thread and hand-sewing needle
- Seam ripper
- One set of $^1/_2$" sew-on black Velcro dots
- Sharp scissors
- Hot iron
- Sewing machine (optional)

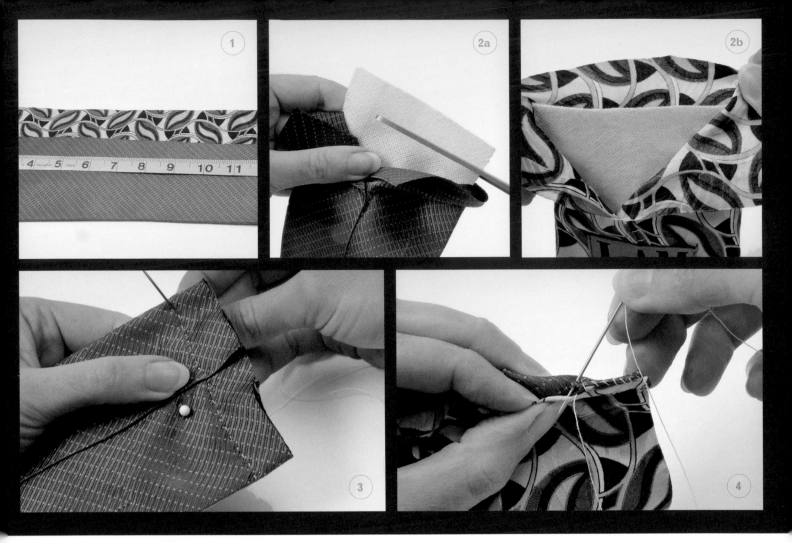

1. You'll need two neckties to make up the body of your wallet. Cut each one 12" from its tip. If any labels are sewn to the back of these neckties, remove them with a seam ripper.

2a and 2b. At the cut end of each necktie, open up the silk outer fabric so that you can access the interior padding fabric. Trim 3/4" off the padding in each necktie and return the silk fabric to its original position.

3. Place the two necktie pieces so that the front sides of the neckties are together. Sew the two pieces together either by hand or by machine, using a 1" seam allowance.

4. Fold both seam allowances inward toward each other so that the raw edges are hidden, and press in place. Hand-sew the seam allowances together at these folded edges using a tiny whipstitch.

5. Decide which of your neckties will form the inside of your wallet. Fold the pointed end of this tie over toward the back, and hand-sew the point in place with tiny whipstitches.

6. Lay the joined neckties on a flat surface, back sides together and the remaining pointed end toward your left, as shown. Line up the bottom edges of the neckties and pin them in place. Then hand-sew the two ties together along this bottom edge, using tiny whipstitches.

7. Sew the hemmed edge of the inside necktie down to the outside necktie. This creates a large interior money pocket for your wallet.

8. Make a pocket or two for credit cards by cutting a 4$\frac{1}{4}$" strip from the leftover skinny end of either necktie. Finish off the cut ends as follows: First, trim out $\frac{1}{2}$" of the internal padding as you did in Step 2; then turn the raw edges of the silk toward the inside and press in place. Use tiny whipstitches to sew around three sides of this piece, attaching it to the inside of your wallet.

(continued)

9. Fold the wallet in half, as shown. Fold the pointed tip of the outside necktie around to the back, and sew on a Velcro dot to close the wallet. Because the neckties are tapered, a little bit of the inner necktie will show at the back of the wallet.

10. Using a seam ripper, remove the center back stitching that holds your third necktie together. Remove and discard the inner padding, and iron the outer silk flat. Cut that silk into squares and make a flower, using the Basic Instructions in Chapter 2.

11. Tack the finished flower to the front panel of the wallet by placing a small dot of fabric glue on the back of the flower and then adhering to the wallet. Allow the glue to dry.

12. Use tiny whipstitches to sew the edge of each flower petal to the wallet.

You should have plenty of necktie material left over to make this cute choker. Simply cut the length you need from the skinny end of the necktie so that it fits comfortably around your neck. Use the method in Step 2 to trim out some padding and then hem the cut end of the necktie. Then use some leftover fabric from this tie to make a flower. Glue your flower to the pointed end of your choker with fabric glue, and then sew on Velcro dots as a closure.

Or, Try This...

Bloomin' Cute Drawer Knobs

Imagine these little flowers on your dresser drawers or your desktop storage chests. You could even use them on cupboard doors. They're tempered with fabric stiffener and then sealed, so they'll stand up to lots of handling.

Before You Begin

- Fabric stiffener is available at large craft stores; just be sure to follow the instructions on the package carefully. You can also use liquid starch.
- Since drawer knobs are handled frequently, you'll want to apply several coats of clear sealer to the Kanzashi to protect them from fingerprints and household dirt. I like Plaid's Patricia Nimocks Clear Acrylic Sealer. Follow the instructions on the package carefully, and let dry completely between coats. 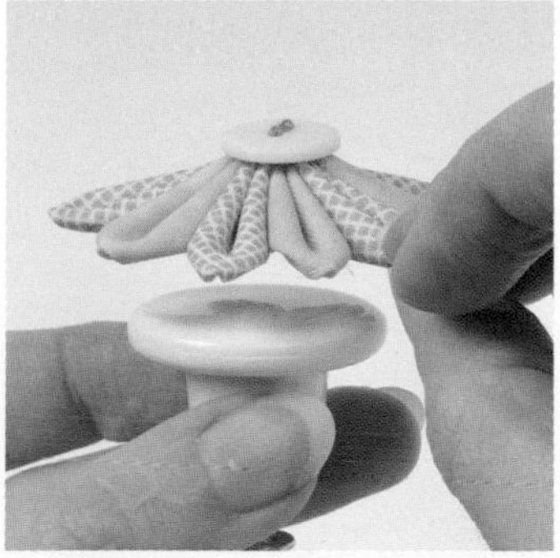
- The hardware we're using for this project is called a "cabinet knob," although you can certainly install it on a drawer!
- Be sure to use a plastic cabinet knob with a flat front, as shown here. We're using E6000 glue to attach the flowers to the pulls because it bonds best to plastic. The flat front is very important in order to allow maximum surface area for the bond.

Skill Level
Intermediate

Best Petal Styles
Pointed

Best Number of Petals
8–10

Best Square Size
2– 2¹/₂"

Glue Needed
E6000

Additional Supplies Needed
- Fabric stiffener (or liquid starch)
- Plastic, flat-front cabinet knob hardware
- Clear matte sealer
- Small paintbrush
- Sharp scissors
- Egg carton (optional)

ASSEMBLING A DRAWER KNOB

1. Make a few test flowers in different fabrics. Brush each one liberally with fabric stiffener (it will soak into the fabric quickly). Allow them to dry for several hours.

2. Flip over each flower to the back and reapply stiffener. Allow them to dry for several hours. Stiffen the front and back a second time and allow to dry so that each flower is completely rigid.

3. Depending on the fabric you've used for your flowers, the stiffener may change the color. This is why test flowers are a good idea. See how different the purple flower on top looks from the one below it? When you have a test flower you like, make one for each drawer pull you need, and repeat Steps 1 and 2 to stiffen them.

4. Use E6000 to attach a center to each flower. (This is a stronger glue than normally used for this step, but these flowers will need to withstand lots of wear.) Allow several hours for the E6000 to set, and then seal each flower on the front and back with several coats of clear sealer. Allow the sealer to dry thoroughly.

5. From this point, complete each knob one at a time. Apply a liberal amount of E6000 to the front of the knob.

6. Firmly press a flower into the glue, centering it on the knob.

7. E6000 takes up to twenty-four hours to dry completely. It's a good idea to stand your drawer knobs in an egg carton so that the pieces won't slide apart while they dry. Let them dry completely before installing them on a drawer or cupboard.

Take a tiny flower, stiffen it, and you have the makings of a very cute zipper pull. You might also like to try stiffening the flowers when you make any of the jewelry projects in this book, especially a pendant or brooch.

Or,
Try This...

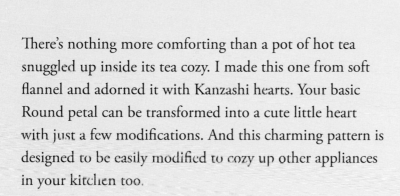

I Heart Tea Cozy

There's nothing more comforting than a pot of hot tea snuggled up inside its tea cozy. I made this one from soft flannel and adorned it with Kanzashi hearts. Your basic Round petal can be transformed into a cute little heart with just a few modifications. And this charming pattern is designed to be easily modified to cozy up other appliances in your kitchen too.

Before You Begin

- If you like, you can also start with a ready-made tea cozy and embellish it with hearts.
- Be careful with fabric-marking pens and pencils: Usually, the heat from your iron will set the marks so they can't be removed later. Follow the package instructions for your marker.
- All seam allowances are 1/4" for this project unless otherwise specified.

Skill Level
Advanced

Best Petal Styles
Round

Best Number of Petals
2 for each heart

Best Square Size
3¹/₂"

Glues Needed
Hot glue, fabric glue

Additional Supplies Needed
- Two colors of coordinating flannel, ¹/₂ yard each
- Scraps of fabrics you plan to use for the hearts and trim
- Coordinating thread for both flannel colors
- Hand-sewing needle
- Straight pins
- Two sets of dressmaker's snaps, size 2
- Measuring tape
- Ruler
- Washable fabric-marking pencil
- Sharp scissors
- Hot iron
- Sewing machine

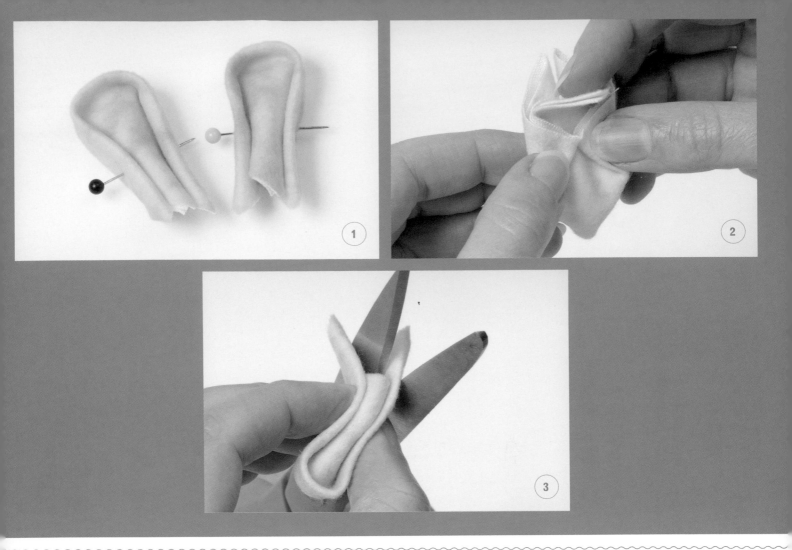

MAKING A HEART

1. Start with two Round petals, held in place with pins. We're going to alter them a little in order to create the heart shape.

2. Take a petal and remove its pin, holding its shape with your fingers. Flip it over to the back and hold it so that the bottom of the petal faces upward. Unfold the center back fold for a moment, and then fold down the layer of the bottom that's closest to you, as shown. Then refold the center back fold.

3. Turn the petal around toward the front. Trim off one of the remaining flaps from the bottom of the petal, as shown. In this example, we've trimmed off the right-hand flap. When you alter the second petal, you'll need to trim off the left-hand flap instead.

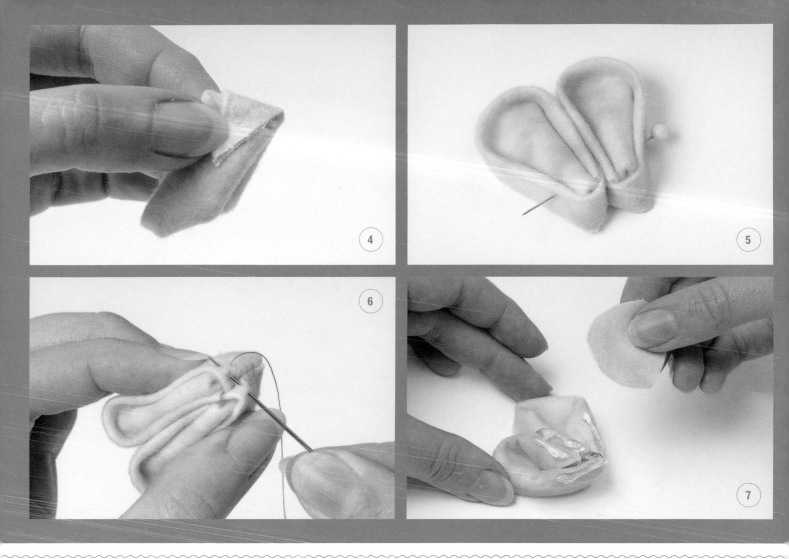

4. Take the remaining long flap that's sticking out from the base of the petal and wrap it around the bottom of the petal, as shown, then pin in place. Repeat Steps 2–4 to alter the second petal. Make sure they're opposite each other: One should have its left-hand side wrapped around the base, and the other should have its right-hand side wrapped around the base.

5. Pin the two petals together, as shown. The flaps you folded around the bases of the petals in Step 4 should now be hidden between the petals.

6. Pinching the two petals together as you sew, stitch the bottom tips together with a tiny whipstitch. Knot the thread securely.

7. Cut a teardrop from the same fabric. This piece will help stabilize the back of the heart. Its shape doesn't have to be precise as long as it covers most of the back, as shown, and isn't visible from the front. Apply hot glue to the center and bottom edges of the heart, as shown, and press the fabric teardrop over the glue.

MAKING A TEA COZY

1. First, measure your teapot to determine the size to cut your fabric. Measure around the circumference of the teapot itself, not including the spout or handle. (You can add 2" for the width of the spout.) Divide this measurement by two, and then add 2". This will be the length of the rectangle you'll cut from your flannel. (For example, my teapot measures 22" around, including the 2" I estimated for the spout. So, 22 divided by 2 is 11. Adding another 2" makes it 13".)

2. Now measure up and over the top of your teapot, starting from the tabletop on one side and ending at the tabletop on the other side. Make sure the tape measure wraps over

the teapot at its tallest point. Divide this measurement in half, and then add 2". This will be the width of the rectangle you'll cut from your flannel. (My teapot measures 15" over its top. Divide that by 2 and you get 7^1/$_2$". Add 2" and you have 9^1/$_2$".)

3. Cut out two rectangles from the flannel you plan to use as the outer layer of your cozy, using the dimensions you calculated in Steps 1 and 2. (My rectangles are 13 × 9^1/$_2$".) Place one of these rectangles on a flat surface, positioned so that it's longer than it is wide. Now divide this rectangle into quarters. A simple way to do this is with an iron: Fold the rectangle in half crosswise and iron a little crease into

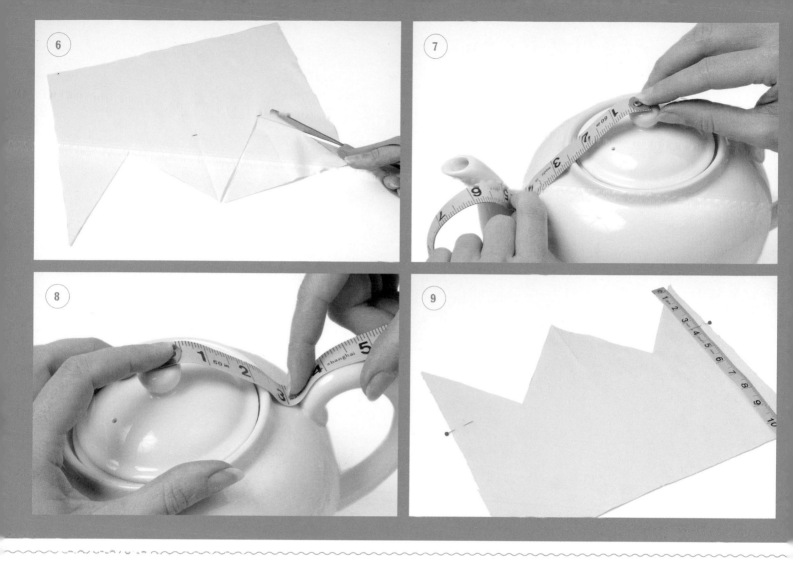

the tip of the fold. That crease marks the center. Fold it in half again and iron another little crease in the tip of that fold. Now your rectangle is divided into quarters. Then flatten it out again.

4. Use a ruler and fabric-marking pencil to mark the wrong side of the fabric 4" from the top of the rectangle at each crease.

5. Using these creases and marks as a guide, mark a deep zigzag along the top of the fabric. Make sure you have high points at the two ends, as shown.

6. Cut along the zigzag lines you've drawn. Repeat Steps 3–6 with the other fabric rectangle.

7. Before sewing these two rectangles together at the sides, take a few more measurements from your teapot. First, measure from the tip of the lid to the base of the spout, as shown. (On my teapot, that's 4".)

8. Next measure from the tip of the teapot lid to the base of the handle, as shown. (On my teapot, that's 3".)

9. Place the two rectangles together with right sides facing each other, matching up all the edges. Now transfer the measurements from Steps 7 and 8 to these rectangles. Measuring from the top, place a pin at the Step 7 measurement on one side of the rectangle. Place a second pin at the Step 8 measurement on the other side.

(continued)

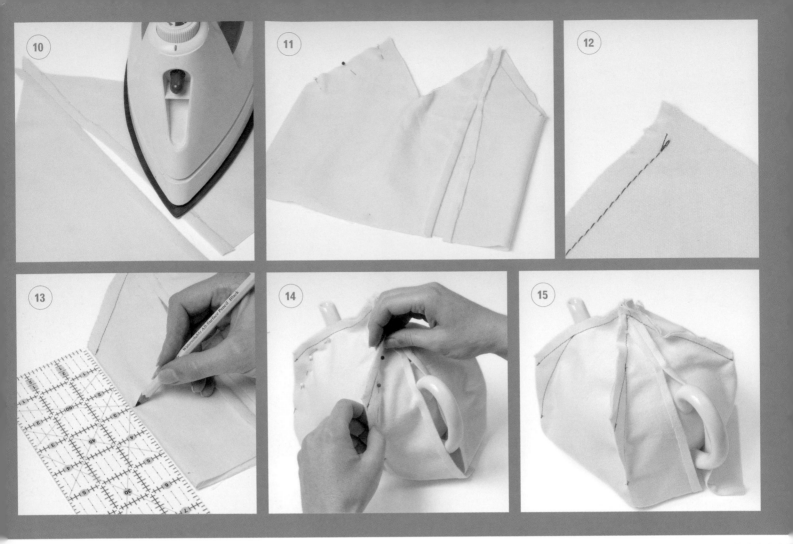

10. Machine-sew the two rectangles together at the sides, starting at the top and stopping at the pins you placed in Step 9. The sides of the cozy should be partially open in order to accommodate the handle and spout of the teapot. Press open both the seams and the seam allowances below the seams.

11. Now make the rounded top of the cozy. Match up the edges of one of the V-cuts you made in Step 6 and pin them together, right sides together.

12. Sew them together, beginning at the base and stopping ¼" short of the top, as shown. Repeat Steps 11 and 12 with the remaining three edges of the top.

13. Now your cozy has four corners. Measure and mark a point 3" down from the edge of each corner, as shown.

14. Tailor your cozy to your teapot. Put the cozy over the teapot, inside out, and fold under the bottom edges until they're flush with your work surface. (This is only to get them out of your way for the moment; no need to pin them.) Next pinch the corners with your fingers so you can see the contour of the teapot underneath. Pin the fabric together along this curve, stopping at the mark you made in Step 13. Repeat this process with the other three corners.

15. Sew along this curve at all four corners, beginning at the original seam line, following your pins, and ending at the mark you made in Step 13. Trim away the excess seam allowance and clip it a few times with scissors to make the curve smoother.

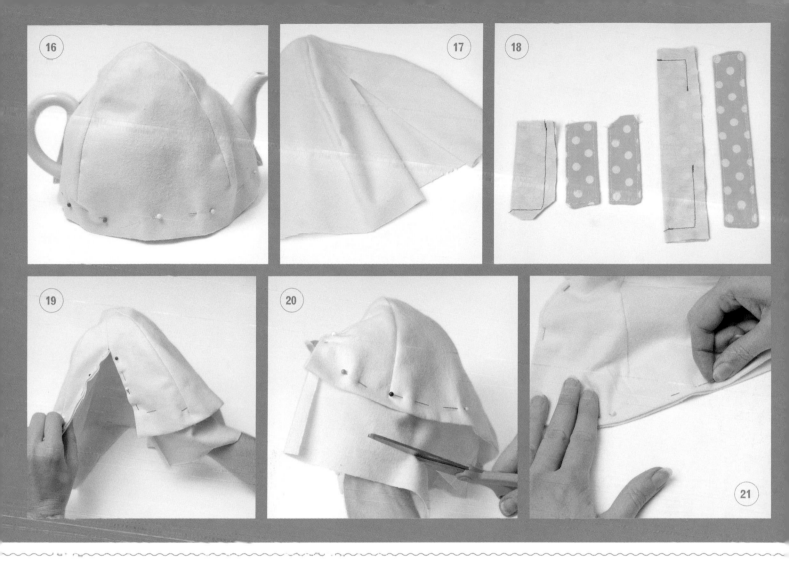

16. Turn the cozy right-side out and press it. Place it back on the teapot. Fold under the bottom edges so that they meet your work surface, as shown. Pin this hem in place and press it, but don't sew it yet.

17. Repeat Steps 3–16 to make a lining from contrasting flannel for your tea cozy.

18. Make two tabs and a tie handle for your cozy as well. For the tabs, cut two 3 × 2¹⁄₂" rectangles, fold each one in half along the 3" edge, and machine-sew, as shown. Clip the corner and turn right-side out. For the tie handle, cut a 3 × 7" rectangle. Fold it in half lengthwise and stitch together, as shown. Clip the corners and turn right-side out. Topstitch close to the edges of all three pieces.

19. Place the lining inside the tea cozy, wrong sides together and matching the side seams. Pin the unsewn edges of the side seams together, as shown.

20. Trim the bottom edge of the lining so that it extends about 2" below the hemmed edge of the outer cozy.

21. Turn under the edge of the lining so that its hem matches that of the outer cozy. Press each hem separately, and then pin them together.

(continued)

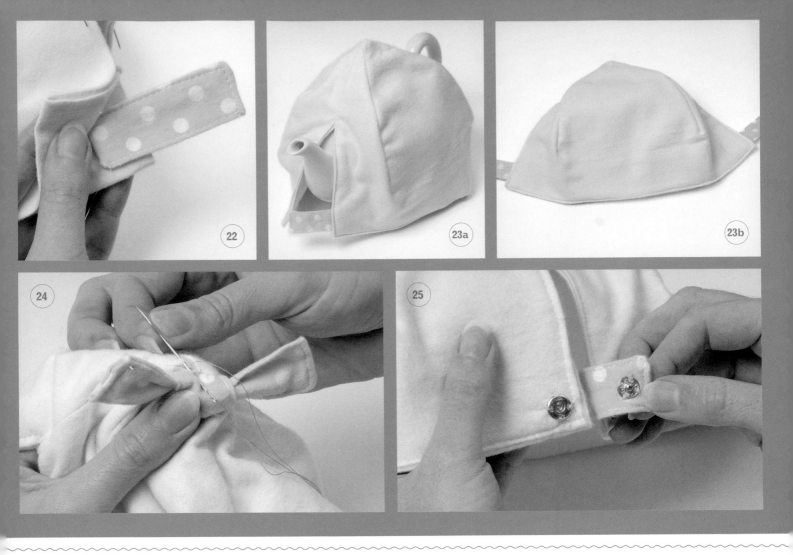

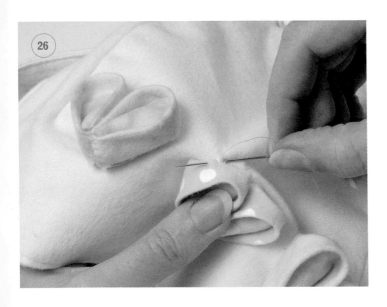

22. Insert a tab between the two layers at each side seam, just above the hem.

23a and 23b. Sew the two layers together by stitching ⅛" from the edges. Your seam will follow the outline of the hem and along the unsewn parts of the side seams.

24. Take the tie handle you made in Step 18 and form it into a loose knot. Attach it to the top of the tea cozy with a tiny whipstitch.

25. Sew a set of snaps to each tab and the cozy, as shown.

26. Attach the hearts to the tea cozy by first tacking them in place with fabric glue and allowing them to dry. Then stitch around the edges of each heart, as shown.

Of course, you can also make Kanzashi flowers out of flannel! Here are two coffee cozies: one for your grinder and one for your French press coffeepot, adapted from this same pattern. And of course, the hearts could be applied to most of the other projects in this book in place of flowers.

Or, Try This...

RESOURCES

Your local craft and fabric stores should have all the supplies you need in order to make basic Kanzashi flowers. Here are a few online manufacturer and wholesaler sources for help in locating some of the specialty supplies used in this book.

Jewelry Tools, Findings, Hair Clip and Barrette Blanks, and Beading
Fire Mountain Gems
www.firemountaingems.com
800-423-2319

Floral Stamens, Tape, and Stem Wire
Darice
www.darice.com
866-4-DARICE

Drawer Pull Hardware
Amerock
www.amerock.com
800-435-6959

TRADITIONAL KANZASHI

If you want to learn more about Tsumami Kanzashi made the traditional way, visit these websites.

Atelier Kanawa
www.atelierkanawa.com
Kuniko Kanawa makes and sells beautiful silk Tsumami Kanzashi. She apprenticed with a master of this art in Japan.

www.youtube.com
Do a search for "Atelier Kanawa" on this video-sharing website to see Kuniko Kanawa explain and demonstrate traditional Tsumami Kanzashi.

Flickr
www.flickr.com
This photo-sharing website is a treasure trove of inspiration. Do a search for "Kanzashi" to see photos of Japanese geisha and maiko wearing them, as well as elegant handmade Tsumami Kanzashi.

Hanatsukuri
www.hanatsukuri.etsy.com
Meghan Willett makes and sells lovely modern Kanzashi based on traditional designs.

Kanzashi Garden
www.kanzashigarden.com
A fantastic informational website about Kanzashi culture and history.

YouTube
www.youtube.com
Do a search for "Tsumami Kanzashi" or "Kanzashi" on this website to find a number of how-to videos for the traditional technique.

ACKNOWLEDGMENTS

I'm indebted to many for the creation of this book:

Kate McKean, who contacted me one day and said, "What about a book on Kanzashi?" and who then proceeded to be one fabulous agent.

Susan Beal, whose advice and friendship have been invaluable to me in so many ways.

Kuniko Kanawa and **Meghan** and **Tara Willett**, who graciously contributed their perspectives and beautiful photographs.

Pam Harris, who took the excellent step-by-step photos throughout this book, fed me during its writing, and taught me to make beautiful things in the first place.

Kirby Harris, who hauled a great deal of photo equipment, drove endless miles, provided technical expertise when needed, and offered unfailing support.

Katin Imes, who took on more than his fair share of household chores, provided even more technical savvy, and never said a word about all the days I wandered around in deadline-wear pajamas and a scary parade-float bedhead hairdo. I love you, Doll!

And if you've ever read my blog, visited one of my classes, or purchased this book, I thank you, too.

AFTERWORD

If you want to go a little deeper into the subject of modern Kanzashi, stop by this book's website, www.kanzashi-in-bloom.com. There you'll find even more links to online Kanzashi resources, plus additional project ideas and places to share the pieces you've created from this book. I would so love to see them!

If you have any questions or comments on the projects in this book, please feel free to contact me through www.kanzashi-in-bloom.com.

INDEX